# Political
# Losers

In Canada, U.S., Ukraine

Michael B. Davie

Manor House Publishing Inc.

National Library of Canada Cataloguing in Publication Data:

Davie, Michael B., 1954-
Political Losers
In Canada, U.S., Ukraine

Includes bibliographical references and notes.

ISBN 0-9685803-7-8

1. Acadians – Expulsion, 1755. 2. Presidents – United States – Election – 1984. #. United States – Politics and government – 1981-1989. 4. Vietnamese Conflict, 1961-1975. 5. Famines – Ukraine – History – 20th Century. I. Title.

D21.3.D35 2001    320.9    C2001-903927-1

Copyright 2001-10-15
By Michael B. Davie and Manor House Publishing Inc.

Published November 15, 2001
by Manor House Publishing: **(905) 648-2193**

All rights reserved.

First Edition.
Cover Design/illustration: Michael B. Davie.
Technical assistance/realization: Richard Kosydar.

# By Michael B. Davie:

The Late Man MH
A Novel

Following The Great Spirit MH
Exploring Native Indian Belief Systems

Political Losers MH
The Lessons Of Failure

Distant Voices MH
Canadian Politics On the Outside Looking In

Canada Decentralized MH
Can Our Nation Survive?

Quebec and Section 33 MH
Why The Notwithstanding Clause Must Not Stand

Inside the Witches' Coven MH
Exploring Wiccan Rituals

Enterprise 2000 MH
Hamilton, Halton, Niagara Embrace the Millennium

Success Stories BR
Business Achievement in Greater Hamilton

Hamilton: It's Happening* BR
Celebrating Hamilton's Sesquicentennial

MH = Published by Manor House Publishing.
BR = Published by BRaSH Publishing
* = With co-author Sherry Sleightholm

# Belated Credit for Past Work:

Please note: Regarding the books Canada Decentralized, Quebec And Section 33 and Inside The Witches' Coven, all by Michael B. Davie, and Mystical Poetry by Deborah Morrison, Davie should have received credit for the cover design on all four books.

Regarding the book Enterprise 2000: Greater Hamilton, Halton and Niagara embrace the New Millennium, author Michael B. Davie should have received credit for the concept and design of the book's cover.

The cover depicted a limitless horizon with, in the foreground, a New Year's baby seated at a computer with the image repeated endlessly on the computer screen.

Davie also originated the back cover concept of the author leaning on the computer monitor showing the baby image, again repeated endlessly.

Photographer Paul Sparrow should have received credit for bringing these images to realization through his skilful photographic and computer montage work.

**– Manor House Publishing Inc.**

For
Philippa

# Acknowledgements

This book would not have been possible without the thoughtful, analytical works of political scientists more seasoned and insightful than I.

I am grateful for the expert teachings of the political scientists I've cited in this book and for the patient distilling of knowledge by my McMaster University professors who helped me to earn honours degrees in Political Science.

As well, I appreciate the assistance extended by Richard Kosydar and many others, too numerous to mention, in bringing this book to fruition.

My thanks, as always, to my wife Philippa for her constant encouragement and faith in the validity of my misadventures.

- **Michael B. Davie.**

# About the author

One of Canada's most intriguing writers, Michael B. Davie is the author of such critically acclaimed business books as Enterprise 2000 and Success Stories.

The award-winning writer is also the author of nationally important books Political Losers, Canada Decentralized and Quebec & Section 33: Why the Notwithstanding Clause Must Not Stand. He also wrote The Late Man, his 10th book and first novel.

Michael B. Davie is also a journalist with The Toronto Star, Canada's largest newspaper, reaching millions of readers daily.

The author has won dozens of awards for outstanding journalism. His work has also appeared in such major Canadian newspapers as the Halifax Chronicle-Herald, Montreal Gazette, Calgary Herald, Winnipeg Free Press, Edmonton Journal and Vancouver Sun.

Prior to The Star, he was an editor with The Globe and Mail, Canada's national newspaper with coast-to-coast readership.

Previous to The Globe, he spent 17 years with The Hamilton Spectator, where he won 28 journalism awards.

Prior to joining The Spectator, he spent five years with other publications, including the daily Welland Tribune where he was a reporter, columnist and editor.

He also served two years as regional news

editor for one of Ontario's largest chains of community newspapers.

Born in Hamilton in 1954, Michael B. Davie's interest in writing began in early childhood. As a pre-school child, he became withdrawn and was in a state of shock after his parents decided to divorce. During a visit to a community centre, the child opened the door to a room to find child psychologists had been studying him through two-way mirrors.

The young child then began closely observing other children and adults, studying their interaction and watching their stories unfold. By the late 1960s and into the 1970s, while in his teens, he was a contributing writer to counter culture publications.

He turned professional in the mid-1970s as Editor of The Phoenix serving Mohawk College of Applied Arts & Technology where he earned a Broadcast Journalism diploma.

He also holds a Niagara College Print Journalism diploma and degrees in Political Science from McMaster University where he was repeatedly named to the Deans' Honour List and won the Political Science Prize for outstanding academic achievement.

Michael B. Davie currently resides in Ancaster with his wife Philippa and their children Donovan, Sarah and Ryan.

# Contents

Opening Notes

Chapter One
The Acadian Expulsion

Chapter Two
Why The Democrats Lost

Chapter Three
On The Losing End: Vietnam On Film

Chapter Four
Killing Fields: Ukraine Forced Famine

Manor House Publishing Inc.
(905) 648-2193.

# Opening Notes

Defeat can hold valuable lessons on how to survive.

Chief among these lessons is the time-tested adage: Find out what went wrong – and don't let it happen again. Learning from these lessons can turn the losers of yesterday into the winners of today and tomorrow.

We begin with a look at the Acadian expulsion, one of the most tragic episodes in Canadian history.

The lesson in this chapter is that the Acadians felt they could remain neutral and stay oblivious to the dramatic political situation swirling around them. This proved to be their undoing.

Had the Acadians been more politically aware (in fairness they were farmers in an age predating mass communications), they might have been more sensitive to the precarious situation the British faced concerning the threat from France and perhaps offered a pledge of allegiance to keep the Brits happy.

Such a pledge might have stipulated their support would stop short of shooting at fellow Frenchmen but would include the provision of supplies and, perhaps, diplomatic efforts such a proclamation to the French to the effect that the Acadians were content being British subjects and did not need "rescuing."

Instead, the Acadians assumed the British would accept their continued non-allegiance and allow them to carry on farming.

Yes, the British over-reacted. But it's unfortunate little heed was paid to the degree of discomfort the British felt at governing a foreign population – in an area prone to attack – that refused to align itself with the British.

Having said that, it should be noted that today's Acadians are faring well.

Although most of the original Acadians were exiled to Louisiana and elsewhere, some remained in Canada – or later returned here – and their descendents are now custodians of a vibrant and living culture.

These Acadians pose no security threat to Canada: They are in fact Canadians, first and foremost. But these proud Canadian citizens are also proud of their Acadian heritage.

Some of today's Acadians have preserved and restored – with assistance from Canada's federal government – Acadian pioneer villages, which offer visitors insight into early Canadian – as well as Acadian – history. In preserving Acadian culture they are adding to the fabric of Canada's culture. Far from being neutral bystanders, they're active members of Canadian society who retain a distinct identity that complements their Canadian identity.

  We next look at Walter Mondale's loss to Ronald Reagan in the 1984 American presidential race.
 The lesson the Democrats appear to have learned from Mondale's embarrassing defeat is that bland simply doesn't sell. Never has. Never will.
 So, the Democrats went searching for a charisma tic, smooth, effective and engaging communicator – and found one in the form of one William Jefferson Clinton.
 A two-term president, Clinton has a legacy of substance and accomplishment (despite his trivial sex scandal).

  We also revisited the Vietnam War – or at least the Hollywood versions of that horrific enterprise.
 To old adages come to mind: History repeats itself; and: Those who do not learn from mistakes of the past are condemned to repeat them.
 Hopefully those adages will not apply to the United States which, going by its Vietnam movies, has learned little from that conflict and portrays it as a war almost won.
 And we'll examine the Ukrainian Holocaust, the Great Forced Famines that so crippled that nation. All of this and more can be found in the chapters ahead.
- **Michael B. Davie.**

"...a good narrative paper... sorts through the debate over necessity convincingly..."

- McMaster University History Professor Ken Draper critiquing the essay "The Acadian Expulsion: An Unnecessary Measure' by Michael B. Davie.

Chapter One

# The Acadian Expulsion
## An Unnecessary Measure

The 1755 expulsion of the Acadians by the British is widely considered one of the most tragic episodes in Canadian history.

American Henry Wadsworth Longfellow's 1847 poem 'Evangeline' and the song 'Acadian Driftwood by the 1960s-1970s Canadian rock group The Bank are just two examples of past and contemporary artistic works portraying the expulsion as a cruel and tragic act.
While there is broad agreement that the British-ordered expulsion of thousands of French-speaking Acadians was lamentable, the question arises: Was it necessary?

In my view, the 1755 expulsion of the Acadians was not necessary. I'll argue that it was an over-reaction on the part of Britain in response to security concerns arising from the military threat from France.

I will show that there was substantial evidence, even at that time, to suggest the Acadians themselves did not pose any significant threat to Britain's efforts to control the region of Acadia in what is today the Canadian province of Nova Scotia.

Acadia's troubles began in 1604, the moment France established Acadia, its first permanent settlement on the Atlantic coast of North America. The location itself proved to be a source of problems. As historian Douglas Francis, offering a brief synopsis, notes:
> "It's strategic location near the Gulf of St. Lawrence meant that England and France fought continually for its possession. The region changed hands frequently until 1713, when France ceded Acadia to England in the Treaty of Utrecht. For the next half-century, Britain ruled over the colony with its predominantly French-speaking and Roman Catholic population."     1.

It was this frequent changing of hands regarding control of Acadia that led the Acadians to strive to offend neither warring power. In a further summarization of Acadia's situation, Francis adds:
> "The Acadians sought to remain neutral in conflicts between England and France. Initially this was possible, but with the con-

struction of the large French fortress of Louisbourg during the 1720s on Cape Breton Island, and the founding of Halifax in 1749, the situation changed. With the revival of hostility between France and England in 1755, Nova Scotia's Lieutenant-Governor, Charles Lawrence, and his council at Halifax insisted that the Acadians take an unconditional oath of allegiance to the British Crown. When they refused, Lawrence expelled approximately 10,000 French Acadians." 2.

The preceding summary sets our a few of the important dates and events that culminated in the expulsion of the Acadians (estimates vary from around 6,000 Acadians to the 10,000 figure Francis cites). The summary also provides us with a general framework of historical events, which we will now examine in more detail.

Acadia began in 1604 as a tiny French community of around 80 people.
The community was founded by Samuel de Champlain, Jean de Poutrincourt – and Pierre du Gua sieur De Monts, a Protestant merchant who was granted a 10-year fur trade monopoly for the region from Henri IV.
The King granted the monopoly on the understanding De Monts would establish a French colony of Catholics in the area of the Bay of Fundy. 3.

After a disastrous first effort at Ile Saint-Croix

in which half the settlers died from cold and scurvy, a second, successful attempt was made and the colony of Port Royal was established. 4.

In his account of Acadian history, written more than a century ago, Acadian writer and former member of Canadian federal parliament Edouard Richard describes the very modest beginnings of Port Royal, a community that was built in a couple of months. The result was, for the most part, far from impressive. As Richard observes:

> "In the course of the following summer, a few dwelling-houses, a store and a palisade enclosing the whole were put up. Thus was Port Royal founded on the very site (now) occupied by the city of Annapolis." 5.

Richard points out that while the fledgling colony was a fragile affair, it was still seen as a threat to neighbouring, larger colonies in New England.

Reflecting on this situation, Richard offers this view of a struggling Acadia, already beginning to feel the presence of powerful neighbours:

> "Exposed as it was, this feeble colony, separated from Canada by vast distances and impenetrable forests, left to its own resources, without immigration, without assistance proportionate to the dangers of its situation, it was the theatre of perhaps greater vicissitudes of war than have fallen to the lot of any other county in the world." 6.

Richard notes Acadia was continually caught between warring powers. He asserts that Acadia's location alone seemed to invite suspicion and hostility:

> "While on the one hand, it was, or might have been, highly useful to France, on the other, it was a constant menace to the commerce and tranquility of the English colonies. It is there that expeditions of adventurers were organized against the new England colonies; there too, attacks were made upon the French. It was a fine field for organizing, it was equally open to attack. Whether the two nations were at war or at peace, it was often war anyhow in these parts. A grievance or a mere pretext was enough to determine disastrous hostilities. Boston and Acadia sometimes waged war on each other on their own account, in spite of temporary peace and amity between the two crowns; and, what is more, on occasions, Acadia was the scene of prolonged hostilities between the Frenchmen who claimed the right to govern the country." 7.

As fragile and vulnerable to attacks as Acadia was, it was also involved in limited expansionism in its early years.

Another Acadian colony was established at the Ile des Monts Deserts (Mount Desert Island) in what is present-day Maine. Established in 1613, less than 10 years after the founding of Acadia itself, the young community survived only briefly.

In July 1613, Virginian solider of fortune Samuel Argall destroyed the new colony, leaving most of its former inhabitants to return to France while a few resettled at Port Royal.     8.

The Argall attack was just one example of numerous attacks to befall Acadia throughout its troubled history.

As historian Naomi Griffiths has noted, Acadia existed within ill-defined boundaries between the expanding empires of New France and New England.

As Griffiths observes, the Acadians responded to this precarious situation be adopting the outlook of "border people" more interested in tending their farms than in dealing with political situations over which they had no control.     9.

In 1621, England's territorial claim on Acadia – which it renamed Nova Scotia – began a long practice of Acadia changing hands between France and England with neither nation having much of an impact on the day-to-day lives of the Acadians who, even as late as the 1670s, numbered fewer than 500 people on peninsular Nova Scotia although tiny settlements would also be established on Prince Edward Island and New Brunswick.     10.

But the French were not the only nation influencing the course of Acadian history. As Griffiths notes:

> "By the end of the century, the Acadians had known one lengthy and legitimate period of English rule, 1654-1668, as well as a number of much shorter periods of English control as a result of raids out of Massachusetts." 11.

The presence of French Acadians so close to the colonies of New England was a source of constant friction from an expansionist Massachusetts. It captured the Acadian capital of Port Royal in the 1670s via an expedition led by William Phipps. 12.

John Clarence Webster, the late president of the Canadian Historical Association, suggests Massachusetts' capture of Port Royal was based on security concerns and was likely part of a boarder agenda:

> "Like the other American colonies, she was anxious about the growing power of France in Canada, and it was her ambition to carry out 'The Glorious Enterprise' proposed about this time by Peter Schuyler of Albany, which had for its aim the extermination of French authority on the continent." 13.

In 1706, the Acadian capital of Port Royal, then under control of the French, came under the leadership of Governor Subercase during a period when animosity against Acadia was running high.

Although the Acadians themselves were not known for widespread acts of piracy or warfare, they regularly supplied neighbouring bands of Indians with firearms that were used in raids on New England colonies. As historian James Hannay notes, the colonies not only blamed Acadia for these raids, but also for a series of raids originating from New France. 14.

A force consisting of English and New England volunteers attacked Port Royal, unsuccessfully at first. But the joint forces subsequently captured Acadia in 1710, a victory, which exposed the poverty within the Acadian colony at a time when France was close to bankruptcy.

Seizure of Acadia by England was officially recognized under the Treaty of Utrecht of 1713. 15.

Although the Treaty of Utrecht formally gave Acadia to England for all time, the Acadians themselves can be forgiven if they didn't appreciate the full significance of this historic document. As Griffiths notes:

> "By 1700, the Acadians were almost as accustomed to dealing with the officials of England as those of France. Thus the defeat of Subercase in 1710 and the subsequent transfer of the colony once more to English control by the Treaty of Utrecht, was, for the Acadians, yet another step in a complicated ritual, an exchange of control over them from France to England, something that had happened be-

fore... and something that would probably be reversed in the not too distant future." 16.

In fact, as Griffiths further observes, the transfer of Acadia between the leading powers of the day was a way of life in the little colony, although it was to have fatal consequences:

> "This fundamental belief in the mutability of power, this dominant sense of the probability of alternate French and English control of the colony, became the cornerstone of Acadian politics during the years 1713 to 1748. It was the basis for Acadian action to refuse requests made by the English officials that they swear an oath of allegiance to the King of England. From the Acadian viewpoint, it would have been folly indeed to engage in any action which would bind them irrevocably to one Great Power when the other was not only obviously in the neighbourhood, but more obviously still interested in the future status of the colony and its inhabitants. Thus the Acadians built a policy compounded of delay and compromise. The oath of George I was rejected outright. Later on, oaths were taken to George II. but in such circumstances as to enable Acadians to believe they had been granted the right to remain neutral." 17.

Given Acadia's status as a tiny, underpopulated colony compared with its neighbours, and the Acadians' long history as a pawn passing between powerful nations, the people of Port Royal understandably wanted to avoid coming into direct conflict with far more powerful forces.

As Griffiths points out, neutrality was Acadia's policy, borne of practical concerns:

> "However it might have looked to outsiders, the question of neutrality was serious enough to the Acadians. it was in fact a consistent policy that was first enunciated in 1717 by the Acadians of Annapolis Royal and later adhered to be them and others in time of war. On being asked for an oath of allegiance to George I, the response of Annapolis Royal (Port Royal) Acadians was a refusal, the reasons given being the matters of religious freedom were not yet clarified and danger from Indians, who were bound to disapprove of friendship between Acadian and English, led to fears for Acadian security. 'Nevertheless.' the response continued, 'we are ready to take an oath that we will take up arms neither against his Britannic Majesty nor against France, nor against their subjects or allies." 18.

As American historian John Bartlett Brebner has pointed out, the practice of both the English and the French referring to Acadians from 1730 onward as 'les francais neutres' or 'the Neutral French' suggests that the neutrality of the Acadians was generally tolerated, if not warmly accepted, by English and French alike.     19.

The Treaty of Utrecht in 1713 changed the balance of power in North America by transferring the French territories of Hudson Bay, Newfoundland and Acadia to England.

Yet it left present day Cape Breton Island and Prince Edward island in French hands, a provision which kept a door open for French expansionism in North America. France wasted little time in taking full advantage of the treaty to build the threatening fortress of Louisbourg. As historian James Hannay notes:
> "The way was thus left clear for France to erect new and powerful establishments on the very borders of Acadia and to retain for herself, the rich fisheries of the Gulf of St. Lawrence, and the political control of the coasts washed by the mighty sea. That was what France immediately proceeded to do. There on the shores of the English harbour began the erection of a great fortress, from which France might look forth and defy her enemies, the widely famed and potent Louisbourg." 20.

Further complicating matters was the fourteenth article of the treaty, which allowed the Acadians freedom of religion, a measure used by the French to plant priest-agitators in the midst of Acadians to sow unrest. The treaty also contained a provision allowing the Acadians up to a year to leave with their possessions should they wish to leave the colony. 21.

Historian Duncan Campbell describes post-treaty Acadia as a land fraught with problems for Britain which began to consider the possibility of removing the Catholic and French Acadians and thus end the difficulties inherent in governing a land where the inhabitants spoke a different language and practiced a different religion and also outnumbered the local British garrisons charged with keeping the peace in Acadia. British distrust of Acadians deepened with a refusal of Acadians to swear unconditional oaths of allegiance to Britain.    22.

However, Campbell also notes that considerations of removing the French Acadians in 1717 and again in 1720 were stalled following strong arguments against such a move from former garrison commander Colonel Samuel Vetch and later from Acadian Governor Richard Philips.

Neither man considered the Acadians a significant threat to security.

Instead, both men expressed concerns that any large departure of Acadians would likely end up at Cape Breton Island where they would bolster the already strong French threat posed by Louisbourg.

As well, the argued, a massive departure of Acadians and their livestock would crush the colony's economy, destroy the local fur trade and disrupt sources of food and labour needed to sustain the British garrison.    23.

In fact, when a number of Acadian families decided to leave Acadia during the first year of the treaty, Governor Philips came up with a range of obstacles intended to keep them in Acadia – such as not allowing them to depart on British vessels – so that they would continue farming the rich lands they had reclaimed from the sea. To accommodate the Acadians, Philips let them swear an oath of non-aggression – not allegiance – regarding Britain. 24.

Griffiths points out that for the most part, the majority of Acadians were neutral and resisted the constant efforts of the nearby French at Louisbourg and invitations from French priests (often suspected of being French agent-agitators) to take up arms against the British or play some other active role in removing the British from Acadia.

Instead, the Acadians continued to walk the tightrope of neutrality. This neutrality worked not only to the advantage of the Acadians, but also to the advantage at times of the English governors of the colony. For example, Griffiths recounts this episode involving Lieutenant-Governor Paul Mascarene's gratitude towards a majority of Acadians who refused to take part in French attacks on the British at Acadia:

"In 1744 when hostilities broke out between English and French in North America, Mascarene, then the lieutenant-governor of the colony, wrote to his masters in London: 'These latter (i.e., the French inhabitants) have given me assurances of their resolution to keep in their fidelity to his Majesty'. Mascarene was convinced that had the Acadians not remained neutral during the hospitalities, the colony would have fallen to the French." 25.

Simply put, the Acadians themselves were instrumental in keeping Acadia in British hands. Griffiths adds:
> "There is no doubt that between 1713 and 1748, the majority of Acadians strove to live on their land truly as neutrals, giving loyalty to neither French nor English. This policy procured for their communities nearly thirty-five years of peace, but its final failure in 1755 has overshadowed its earlier success. it was a policy that produced peace and quiet for the Acadian communities, however catastrophic it finally proved to be." 26.

In 1748, however, the Acadians' situation changed for the worse.

The Treaty of Aux-la-Chapelle ended hostilities between France and Britain.

But it returned to the French, the fortress of Louisbourg, which had been captured by a band of New Englanders in 1745.

The return of the French fortress revived an old threat and inflamed security concerns of New

Englanders, prompting Governor Shirley of Massachusetts to call for the removal of the French influence in the area. In particular, Shirley called for the expulsion of Acadians and their replacement by British immigrants.     27.

In 1749, the British founded Halifax, made it the capital of Nova Scotia and immediately sent 2,000 immigrants from England and New England to populate it. An additional 1,500 immigrants from Germany soon followed, giving the British an overnight population of hand-picked citizens  nearly half the population of the Acadians who numbered 8,000 in 1749.

Governor Cornwallis demanded an oath of allegiance fro the Acadians but did not press the matter when they refused. His successor, Governor Hopson, did not ask for the oath and Acadians remained neutral.    28.

At this point, let me suggest that any remaining perceived threat from Acadians could have been erased in short order by allowing additional waves on non-Acadian immigration to take place, giving the British an overwhelming numerical advantage.

But although further immigration did indeed take place, peaceful coexistence with the Acadians was not to be: In 1753, Charles Lawrence was appointed governor and he envisioned a Nova Scotia that was capable of surviving and thriving without Acadians.

Lawrence was actively considering expelling the Acadians when hostilities broke out between England and France in 1754 and British forces succeeded in capturing the French fort Beausejour.    29.

Then, in 1755, Lawrence ordered Acadians to swear an oath of unconditional allegiance to England.

When most Acadians predictably refused to take the oath, Lawrence ordered all Acadians – including those who did take the oath – deported. Thousands of Acadians were loaded onto waiting boats and taken to pre-arranged destinations – such as Louisiana – during the years 1755 to 1763.    30.

Historian Francis Parkman, writing in 1884, offers a rare view I have not encountered elsewhere: He suggests Lawrence had little choice but to expel the Acadians. Parkman would have us believe:
> "Whatever judgement may be passed on the cruel measure of wholesale expatriation, it was not put into execution till every resource of patience and persuasion had been tried in vain."    31.

This brief assertion has been strongly rejected, not only by myself, but by a number of prominent historians, including Richard, who notes Parkman has overlooked a number of important historical documents along with evidence showing that the vast majority of Acadians had never taken up arms against the British – even when it would have been to their possible advantage to do so. This recalls the Acadians' refusal to aid the French against Mascarene when such assistance would have likely ousted the British from Acadia.

Richard also notes the Acadians willingly turned over their weapons to the British, who were surprised to find more than 2,000 hunting rifles in their midst. Richard asks:
> "What was to be feared now that they were deprived of them and that surrender of these arms had been effected without resistance, everywhere, upon a mere command? How could they be dangerous when their boats had been confiscated and when the French had been expelled from al of their strongholds on the coast? Let Mr. Parkman answer this question, he, who in order to prejudge the matter, has not so much as alluded to the seizure of arms and boats, he who has carefully eschewed whatever could throw light on this ignoble tragedy." 32.

Richard also draws attention to the governor's own correspondence in which he indicates that plans for an expulsion had been well developed for some time in advance of the oath-ultimatum being given. In other letters, Lawrence expresses doubts the Acadians would ever take up arms against the British.

Yet Lawrence also expresses hope the Acadians will refuse to take the oath so he can deport them. 33.

Historian W. J. Eccles notes the expulsion is particularly controversial because it took place after the British had captured Fort Beausejour at the foot of the Bay of Fundy and thus had removed the French threat in Nova Scotia.

Eccles also suggests the severity of the fate dealt the Acadians only served to galvanize French resistance in Quebec, making the French there determined to fight hard to prevent a similar fate from ever befalling them.     34.

Historian George Frederick Clark, similarly suggests the expulsion wasn't necessary and indicates the decision had a lot to do with the character of Lawrence, a poorly educated and widely disliked man who rose from humble beginnings to hold the a position requiring a degree of sensitivity and statesmanship he simply did not possess.
Clark notes Lawrence was hated, not just by the Acadians, but by many in Halifax who devoted passages of their correspondence to describing Lawrence's arrogant nature, his vile disposition and his inability to tolerate anyone who opinion differed from his own.

As well, Clark observes Lawrence had stated beliefs to the effect that the Acadians posed no real threat.

Finally, there is the complete lack of any statement of sympathy or empathy by Lawrence toward the Acadians, before, during or after their expulsion, which Clark suspects was a decision driven largely by Lawrence's vile nature.   35.

Whether the decision to expel thousands of Acadians was largely driven by any perverse nature on the part of a former governor is open to interpretation.

My own reading of this situation is that Lawrence's nature did indeed play a major role in the expulsion.

However, what the evidence cited throughout this essay makes abundantly clear is that the decision itself was not necessary.

As demonstrated, based on the works of various prominent historians, the vast majority of Acadians had peacefully co-existed with the British for many decades and only a small minority of Acadians had ever resorted to any form of armed resistance or provided any assistance and arms to enemies of the British.

Considering that the Acadians were French-speaking Catholics with relatives in New France and France, the neutrality they offered the British was likely the best possible arrangement the British could have hoped for.

The Acadians could not have reasonably been expected to take up arms against their French kin.

Instead, the Acadians offered – and kept – assurances that they would fight neither British nor French.

This neutrality was accepted and appreciated by more than one governor, especially Mascarene, who openly admitted the colony would have been captured by the French during his tenure had the Acadians broken their neutrality to side with the French.

Indeed, throughout much of their co-existence with the British, the Acadians could have presented a threat if they had wanted to do so.

The Acadians came to number in the thousands and were well stocked with more than enough rifles to conquer the small British garrison of around 200 men who presided over Acadia for decades.

Instead, the Acadians largely preferred to farm their lands in peace.

Evidence cited by historians indicates the expulsion was an unnecessary, pre-meditated act, which used the excuse of a refused oath to justify its execution.

Of course, the Acadians had refused similar unconditional oaths in the past and this position of neutrality had always been accepted.

As Clarke notes, Lawrence was actually expecting – even hoping – the Acadians would give him the excuse he needed to expel them.

The Acadians, who had for years resisted French efforts to entice them to attack the British, were expelled at a time when they presented so threat at all to the British.

The region was controlled from its new capital of Halifax and rapid waves of British immigration were beginning to rival the Acadians as the dominant population in Nova Scotia. Given a short period of time, it was likely the British in Nova Scotia would have enjoyed numerical superiority over the Acadians thus removing any threat from a people who had never presented a threat – even when they dominated the landscape.

With Britain having emerged victorious from the 1750s hostilities and having captured all French forts in peninsular Nova Scotia, Britain also removed a source of French agitators – who'd never successfully enticed the Acadians to attack the British.

Of course, the minority of Acadians who were guilty of crimes against the British could have been dealt with judiciously without Lawrence ever having to expel the entire, largely peaceful population (including those who had taken the oath of allegiance).

The Acadians' lengthy, peaceful history of non-violent coexistence with the British, their refusal to accept French invitations and threats to attack the British, their role as a supplier of food and labour to a vulnerable garrison, their honoured pledges of neutrality, their refusal to use their thousands of guns against the British and their acceptance of British rule combined with Britain's eventual position of extreme dominance in the region of New England, northward, all lead to the inescapable conclusion that the expulsion simply wasn't necessary.

That the expulsion took place was enough to render the Acadians political losers.

However, it should be noted that the expelled Acadians simply went on to enrich the culture of Louisiana (while impoverishing Canada's culture).

It should also be noted that the ascendants of the expelled Acadians have found a way to preserve their old culture – and contribute to Canada's overall culture – and that these loyal Canadians pose no threat whatsoever to Canada. Acadia lives on today as a valued region of Canada.

# End Notes

1. Francis, Douglas R., and Donald B., Readings in Canadian History: Pre Confederation, Holt, Rinehart and Winston, 1990. p. 147.
2. IBID
3. Daigle, Jean, Historical Synthesis: 1604-1763. The Acadians of the Maritimes, Centre d'etudes acadiennes, Moncton, NB, 1982. p. 32
4. IBID
5. Richard, Edouard, Acadia: Missing Links of a Lost Chapter in American history, New York Home Book Company, John Lovell and Son, Montreal, 1985. p. 27.
6. IBID
7. IBID
8. Daigle, Jean, Historical Synthesis: 1604-1763. The Acadians of the Maritimes, Centre d'etudes acadiennes, Moncton, NB, 1982. p. 20
9. Griffiths, Naomi, E.S., The Acadian Deportation: Deliberate Perfidy or Cruel Necessity?, Copp Clark Publishing Co., Toronto, 1969. p. 2.
10. IBID
11. Griffiths, Naomi, E.S., The Golden Age: Acadian Life, 1713-1748, Social History 17, 33 (May 1984) pp. 21-34.

12. Webster, John Clarence, Acadia and the End of the Seventeenth Century, Tribune Press, Sackville, NB, '34. p.2
13. IBID
14. Hannay, James, The History of Acadia from its First Discovery to its Surrender to England, J&A McMillan, St. John, NB, 1879. pp 265-269.
15. IBID pp 269-281.
16. Griffiths, Naomi, E.S., The Golden Age: Acadian Life, 1713-1748, Social History 17, 33 (May 1984) pp. 21-34.
17. IBID
18. IBID
19. Brebner, J.B,, New England's Outpost: Acadia Before the Conquest of Canada, New York: Columbia University Press, 1927. pp 15-16.
20. Hannay, James, The History of Acadia from its First Discovery to its Surrender to England, J&A McMillan, St. John, NB, 1879. p. 307.
21. IBID p. 308.
22. Campbell, Duncan, Nova Scotia and its Historical, Mercantile and Industrial Relations, Montreal, John Lovell and Sons, 1873. pp 73-80.
23. IBID
24. IBID
25. Griffiths, Naomi, E.S., The Golden Age: Acadian Life, 1713-1748, Social History 17, 33 (May 1984) pp. 21-34.
26. IBID

27. Daigle, Jean, Historical Synthesis: 1604-1763. The Acadians of the Maritimes, Centre d'etudes acadiennes, Moncton, NB 1982. 44-46
28. IBID
29. IBID
30. IBID
31. An excerpt from The Acadian Deportation, N. E. S. Griffiths, Copp Clark, 1969. p. 6.
32. Richard, Edouard, Acadia: Missing Links of a Lost Chapter in American history, New York Home Book Company, John Lovell and Son, Montreal, 1985. pp 30-31.
33. IBID
34. Eccles, W. J., France in America, Harper and Row, 1972, p 17.
35. Clarke, George Frederick, Expulsion of the Acadians, Brunswick Press, Fredericton, NB, 1955. pp 21-27.

"... a very good analysis... excellent emphasis...very good use of quotations..."

- McMaster University Political Science Professor Dr. George Breckenridge critiquing 'Presidential Election 1984: Why The Democrats Lost' by Michael B. Davie.

## Chapter Two

## U.S. Presidential Election 1984:
# Why The Democrats Lost

The Democrats' loss in the 1984 presidential election was attributable to an array of factors.

As this chapter will show, most of these factors were magnified by the Democrats' chief disadvantage: the enormous electoral appeal enjoyed by the incumbent President Ronald Reagan.

Based on analytical writings culled from the books of expert political observers, I will explore the key events, developments and underlying circumstances contributing to Republican President Ronald Reagan's landslide victory over Democratic Party Leader Walter Mondale.

Within this context, we'll examine important contributors to the electoral outcome.

These factors include: Reagan's formidable advantage as the incumbent, the president's mastery of televised communicating, his carefully cultivated strong leader persona, his good fortune at seeking re-election during a period of prosperity and his ability to convincingly tell the American public the optimistic message it wanted to hear.

We'll also probe the factors leading to Mondale's dismal showing at the polls and his crushing electoral defeat.

Factors to be examined here include: Mondale's difficulties with televised communicating, the credibility-damaging blows he sustained in the Democratic Leadership Primaries, Mondale's unenviable catch-up position from the start of this lop-sided presidential contest, his miscued policy pronouncements and his inability to effectively convey an appealing vision of America.

Reagan's victory was truly a landslide: He won 59 per cent of the popular vote in the 1984 U.S. Presidential Election and received a record 525 electoral votes.

In fact, Reagan nearly swept all 50 states in his astonishing – by its sheer magnitude – victory.
The incumbent president lost only two jurisdic-

tions: the state of Minnesota (Mondale's home state) and D.C.   1.

Despite Reagan's age (he was in his 70s) and near-legendary lapses in performance (he once referred to the state of Hawaii as a U.S. "ally" and stupidly joked into an open radio microphone that he was about to commence bombing the Soviet Union), he helped heal the spirit of a deeply troubled, post-Vietnam War America by becoming that nation's biggest feel-good cheerleader.

And it was this remarkable ability to strike a sympathetic, optimistic chord with Americans that propelled Reagan to his landslide victory.

Indeed, Reagan's impressive win was owed in large part to his ability to cheer up a pessimistic nation and tell Americans what they wanted to hear.

As Henry Plotkin, co-author of 'The Election of 1984' recalls:
> "Even Walter Mondale admitted in the first debate that President Reagan had done much to improve the morale of the nation. This was no mean feat in a nation that had suffered through the traumatic '70s of Watergate, Vietnam, double-digit inflation, soaring interest rates and the humiliation in Iran. The simple patriotism of Reagan with its boundless optimism about America's future and glorification of America's past was wel-

comed by a public that had grown weary of years of criticism and self-doubt. The Reagan message played well in America and Succeeded in Altering the way the nation saw itself and its government." 2.

But there was more to Reagan's landslide win than feel-good messages. He took a calculated, two-sided approach.

Another 'Election of 1984' author, Gerald Pomper, refers to this approach and observes:
"Generally, campaigns can be waged on issues or personalities. The Reagan effort used both. The president was credited with achieving prosperity for the nation, with the economy registering an astonishing growth rate of over 10 per cent early in 1984, along with low inflation. In foreign policy, Reagan boasted that "America is back, standing tall," citing the successful American intervention in Grenada and increased military capability." 3.

Plotkin says Reagan's optimistic pronouncements on the United States and an improving economy, eventually paid large dividends at the polls:
"Reagan's success in no small measure was his ability to redirect the memory of many Americans away from painful experiences toward more pleasant ones. As he had done in 1980, Reagan often referred to America as

John Winthrop's 'City Upon A Hill' – the case for American exceptionalism, of an America as "mankind's last, best hope." His success at bringing the economy back to life was used by his supporters as proof of the success of Reagan's philosophy and as a rebuke to welfare state liberalism." 4.

As the incumbent president, Reagan made ready use of televised speeches and commercials depicting himself as a vibrant world leader, comfortably at home in the Oval Office, reflecting on past and present successes.

Public perceptions of increased military prowess, an improving economy, and a confident, effective leader at the helm, all combined to give President Reagan a strong, early advantage in the presidential contest.

In fact, public opinion polls showed many voters in the electorate had already decided to back Reagan without ever giving much thought to Mondale. As Pomper notes:
> "Almost half the voters had made their decision at the beginning of the year, and only a fourth even waited for the televised debates. As a result… there was little change in sentiment over the course of the year. There were some variations, particularly rallies toward Mondale after the first debate. The dominant trend, however, was simple consolidation, as

the electorate… crystallized its sentiments into a rock-hard majority for Reagan." 5.

It was this early strength in the campaign that would eventually generate Reagan's landslide victory. As Pomper adds:
> "The Reagan victory was both broad and deep. Even in Minnesota, the one state he lost, he fell short by only 4,000 votes, a fraction of a percentage point." 6.

Beyond economic and image factors, large numbers of voters were also taken by the incumbent's ideas, his philosophy that America could truly prosper with freer enterprise, less government and more patriotism.

Reagan seemed to personify the hopes and aspirations of the American public. As authors Peter Goldman and Tony Fuller recall in 'The Quest For The Presidency 1984':
> "Reagan sought to consolidate the victory of a new American consensus, a popular ideology built around a core of anti-state and anti-Soviet conservatism and to bequeath the fruits of that victory to heirs in the Republican party. Mondale laboured to make the Democrats competitive again and found himself imprisoned instead in the old days and old ways like a fly in amber." 7.

With the polls also showing a majority of Americans relatively satisfied with the state of the union, Reagan also enjoyed the peculiar advantage of being lionized by the public to the extent that blame for mistakes seemed to roll off of him. As Goldman and Fuller note:

> "His presidency seemed in the apt metaphor of Congresswoman Pat Schroeder of Colorado, to be coated in Teflon; nothing negative ever seemed to stick to him." 8.

Reagan took little blame for failings that included a deficit that ballooned to $200-billion under his presidency. Commenting further on the Teflon factor, Scott Keeter, a co-author of 'The Election of 1984', notes:

> "Reagan was not hurt by the deficit because Mondale failed to pin the blame for it on him. Even though the deficit under Reagan was larger than that accumulated by any other president, half the public blamed "the Democratic Congress," rather than Reagan (30 per cent did blame Reagan). When offered a choice of Reagan or "previous presidents," an even larger portion of the public (60 per cent) blamed Reagan's predecessors. One can hardly find a better manifestation of the 'Teflon presidency'." 9.

Of Reagan's immense popularity, 'Visions Of America' author William A. Henry III observes:

> "From the beginning, the 1984 election was not a race that the Democrats hoped to win. Rather, it was a contest that everyone

acknowledged Ronald Reagan would have to lose, if change was to be." 10.

Further examining the Reagan appeal, William A. Henry III concludes:
> "Reagan appeared to have attained the ultimate goal of every national politician: to embody so thoroughly the myths and traits of the country's idealized image of itself that a vote for Ronald Reagan would be a vote for the real America." 11.

All of this meant Mondale faced an arduous, uphill battle to unseat an enormously popular, blame-shedding incumbent riding a wave of economic prosperity.

In short, Mondale faced a president who was equated with a strong America and who had already won the electorate over with his image and ideas before the contest ever really began.

Against such odds, Mondale needed a nearly flawless campaign and great success at exploiting Reagan's weak points. Neither came about.

As Mondale was preparing to contest the presidency, he was recovering from a series of gruelling Democratic Party leadership primaries, which he won only after sustaining a number of credibility-damaging blows from fellow Democrats competing for the nomination.

Perhaps the harshest of these blows came from rival Colorado Senator Gary Hart who went after Mondale with hard-hitting commercial 'Hart attacks'.

Jack Germond and Jules Witcover, co-authors of the aptly titled 'Wake Us When It's Over', recall one of Hart's nastier attacks:

> "His campaign in New York began to run what became known as "the fuse ad," showing a bomb with a lighted fuse, as a narrator said: "When President Reagan sent men to Central America he called them advisors. Remember Vietnam? Our troops now serve as bodyguards to dictators, and are a slow-burning fuse to war. Vice President Mondale agrees with President Reagan and said he too would leave some of the troops there as bargaining chips with Nicaragua. And he attacks Gary Hart for forcefully saying, "Get them out." Our sons as bargaining chips... Will we never learn?" 12.

Anyone considering the merits of Mondale as a potential president would have found it difficult to forget the lingering, tainted pronouncements Hart had made against Mondale.

Indeed, one of the earliest and most serious obstacles faced by Mondale was the need to overcome his savaged reputation due to image-damaging infighting in the Democratic Party.

In contrast, Reagan, as the incumbent president – and a popular one at that – was spared such scrutiny by his own party.

Reagan could sit comfortably on the sidelines and watch the Democrats attack each others' reputations and place Mondale on the defensive. As Germond and Witcover note:
> "The 1983 preliminaries were all the more self-destructive for the Democrats because their candidates spent almost all that time bickering among themselves about the past. Woe betide the candidate who had cast an incautious vote on some aspect of Reaganomics or failed to pass the litmus test for devotion to arms reduction." 13.

Also in contrast to Reagan and the president's robust image, Mondale's image was decidedly bland. As William A. Henry III observes:
> "Mondale's self-image as a mere inheritor, a placeholder for Roosevelt, was dispiritingly apt. Democrats had no Mondalism to stack up against Reaganism, no movement clamouring for his voice and leadership, no worldview or value system that he alone best expressed. Mondale offered the most practical but least inspirational quality in politics: acceptability... No one told Walter Mondale anecdotes... He had a sound analytical mind, but without a hint of poetry." 14.

Reagan, long-dubbed The Great Communicator, was a former actor and a consummate expert at playing the role of president before the cameras; his voice choking with emotion at the right moment, his face breaking into a strong-jawed grin after sharing a one-liner, his voice forceful and direct when he spoke of America's powerful place in the world.

Again, all of this was in stark contrast to Mondale. As Germond and Witcover note:
> "Against this campaign phenomenon who functioned equally well on platform and on camera, the Mondale campaign had a candidate, who, on the stump came over on his best days as an angry, even petulant, scold and who was extremely uncomfortable appearing on television." 15.

Mondale was an old-style politician who failed to master the art of televised communicating during a modern age when television played, and continues to play, an important role in sending political messages to the masses.

Jonathan Moore, editor of 'Campaign For President', suggests television also manipulates, distorts and hinders substantial information from ever reaching the public intact. As Moore observes:
> "Television, which informs more people faster and more efficiently than ever before, also does so in quick bites, and is prone to the entertainment side of its personal-

ity... Thus, candidates are encouraged to be more superficial and rhetorical – and sometimes artificially dramatic – in response to TV's opportunities and requirements." 16.

Mondale, who preferred campaigning on issues rather than personalities, didn't like television, and, as 'The Presidential Election Show' author Keith Blume says TV – by narrowly focusing on Reagan's lead – was less than kind to Mondale. Blume asserts:
"Every night on the night news programs, image and repetition was the operative approach. Ronald Reagan was The Great Communicator and his re-election was inevitable. Walter Mondale was "boring" and his challenge was impossible. To think that the constant repetition of these images does not have an enormous impact on the electorate would be to have one's head in the sand." 17.

Similarly, a somewhat sparse Labour Day turnout for Mondale should not have particularly hurt the candidate.
But as Germond and Witcover note, television made sure the sparse crowd did hurt Mondale since "through the prism of a television camera's eye, a large crowd helped a politician look successful and a sparse one could suggest failure." 18.

Nor could Mondale, a former long-time supporter of the Vietnam War, sharply differentiate himself Reagan on the arms race against the Communists.

Observer William Henry III said of Mondale:
"In later years he said that his slowness to oppose the conflict had been his greatest public error. It certainly estranged him from a whole stratum of affluent Baby Boom-generation professionals who regarded Vietnam as a better index than Social Security of whether a candidate shared their particular brand of responsible liberalism." 19.

There is also a general consensus among various authors cited in this essay that Mondale erred in his choice of a running mate when he selected Geraldine Ferraro, giving him a difficult –to-win, north-north ticket that undoubtedly cost him support in the American South.

University professors Paul Abramson, John Aldrich and David Rohde, co-authors of 'Change and Continuity in the 1984 Elections', explain the historical weakness of such a ticket when they state:
"The Democrats have won only one presidential election after 1948 with a northern Democrat at the top of the ticket (1960), and none without a southerner on the ticket at all. the reason is that, without any southern electoral votes, it is difficult to put together any conceivable winning coalition. It is not that it was logically impossible for Mondale to win in 1984, but that the combination of events for a win were so unlikely as to make it practically impossible." 20.

Ferraro may have also hindered the Mondale campaign by following Mondale's winning first presidential debate performance against Reagan with her own lacklustre and wooden performance against Vice-President George Bush only days later.

As well, Ferraro was forced into giving a press conference on her family taxes after promising to disclose them.

But that situation went from bad to worse when Ferraro's own husband, John Zaccaro, initially refused to disclose his own taxes. The entire affair had a surreal quality about it that proved costly to the Mondale-Ferraro campaign. The 'Change and Continuity' co-authors add:
> "Beyond the negative publicity, Mondale-Ferraro lost the opportunity to gain ground on Reagan – something candidates so far behind could ill afford." 21.

Mondale appeared to remain intent on telling Americans what they needed to hear rather than what they wanted to hear.

He tried to honestly warn the public of the dangers of massive government debts and he promised a tax hike to slow the debt's growth.

Although this initially surprised the Reagan camp, Reagan soon turned the situation to his advantage and "hammered away repeatedly on the tax issue, stating: "Our friends in the other party have never met a tax they didn't like – they didn't like or hike."   22.

Mondale was widely considered to have lost the second debate after Reagan glibly – and humorously – countered Mondale's suggestions that he was too old to run for president. Reagan stated that he wouldn't make age an issue and would not therefore exploit his opponent's "youth and inexperience." The line drew an endearing laugh from debate watchers – and from Mondale himself. Reagan's comment proved to be pure gold. The incumbent president's clever line also "deftly defused the age issue, and at that moment, for all intents and purposes, the presidential campaign of 1984 was over.   23.

In an effort to make his north-north ticket more appealing to the South, Mondale chose Bert Lance as national party chairman.

But Mondale's move ultimately backfired because it saddled him with Lance's political baggage, including a scandal over charges of banking irregularities by the former Georgia party chairman (although Lance was acquitted of the charges in 1980).

This selection of a "tarnished" chairman alienated some southern supporters and limited Mondale's ability to attack Reagan's conduct as any attack might invite a Lance-inspired return volley from Reagan. Faced with such constraints, Mondale eventually dropped Lance.   24.

Political observer Harold Stanley observed that the nation-wide popularity of Reagan remained a huge obstacle to Mondale, even in the South, once a traditional stronghold of the Democrats. Indeed, Stanley quite neatly summarized some of the factors behind Mondale's failure to do well in the South when he noted:

> "Given Reagan's popularity nationally and within the South, a Mondale victory would have been difficult to achieve. Picking a non-southern, liberal and female running mate; elevating, then dropping Bert Lance; and promising to raise taxes – such moves by Mondale made a difficult campaign even more so in the South. Moreover, most southern Democratic elected officials and leaders refrained from taking an active, visible role on behalf of Mondale." 25.

Stanley suggests that while southern White support for Reagan has been interpreted by some as a backlash against high Black voter registration for the Democrats, this is too simplistic an interpretation, as many voters supported Reagan for entirely different reasons. Stanley asserts:

> "Economic recovery, a strong defence, reviving patriotism, religious emphasis, strong leadership – such themes struck a responsive chord among white southerners." 26.

Mondale did obtain most of the Black vote and while Mondale may have also hoped in vain for record turnouts by this voting group, Stanley suggests an even greater Black voter turnout would likely not have made enough of a difference to significantly change the election outcome. Stanley states:

> "Black voter turnout lagged behind the high expectations fuelled by the registration increases, but since Reagan carried more than 70 per cent of the southern White vote, even higher Black turnouts would not have significantly altered the outcome." 27.

Stanley also observes the South was supposed to have been Mondale's stronghold and the source of his high hopes for election. Unfortunately, nobody told the South:

> "The South did not respond favourably to Mondale and Ferraro. This mirrored the situation in the rest of the nation, but the South had been singled out for special attention and was seen as critical to success. In part, the flaps over Lance's position and Ferraro's finances eclipsed other more favourable focuses." 28.

In the end, Mondale was unable to overcome the strong advantage Reagan had held since the start of the campaign.

Reagan was in a powerful position, an incumbent president riding a wave of economic prosperity and revived patriotism who was virtually assured re-election barring any unforeseen developments.

It would take a very strong opponent to unseat Reagan – and Mondale proved to be an exceptionally weak contender, an awkward old-style politician, hopelessly outmatched by Reagan's mastery of televised communicating and public speaking.

Against Reagan's message of prosperity and patriotism, Mondale offered a message of fearful debts and promised tax hikes.

The only moment in the campaign in which Mondale appeared to have any real chance at all occurred early on during the first televised debate in which Mondale fared better than expected over a decidedly ill-prepared Reagan. By exceeding low expectations, Mondale was deemed to have 'won' that first televised debate.

However, Mondale soon lost this fleeting momentum when Ferraro took her turn at bat and fared poorly in the debate against Vice President Bush.

Mondale then 'lost' the second televised debate when he again went up against Reagan but found the incumbent president to be far better prepared for the second round.

Of course, Mondale also miscalculated badly in his choice of a north-north ticket that did nothing to pull in southern support, then followed this with the ill-fated choice of Lance as campaign chairman.

All of this, combined with an inability to capture the imagination of the South or get its influential Democrats actively involved, left Mondale with a weak showing in what had been traditionally strong Democrat territory (although in fairness to Mondale, this advantage had been in decline since 1964).

To further sum up: Other factors contributing to the Democrats' loss included Ferraro's tax problems, Mondale's formerly conservative position on Vietnam, his arguably boring personality and his difficulties in providing any kind of credible foil against the Great Communicator, Ronald Reagan.

It would have taken a brilliant campaign by Mondale, a stunning personal performance and few mistakes to make inroads against the strong advantages Reagan held at the outset.

But Mondale and the Democrats were unable to mount a serious threat to Reagan's re-election.

The questionable moves by the Democrats only added new factors to the central reason for their failure to win: Reagan's enviable position as a well-liked incumbent president seeking re-election during a period of great prosperity.

While many factors contributed to the Democrats' defeat, the biggest single reason lay with the popularity of the incumbent President Reagan.

Against a powerful tide of Reaganism, Mondale and the Democrats quite simply failed to offer an appealing alternative.

# End Notes

1. Gerald M. Pomper, The Election of 1984: Reports and Interpretations, various authors, edited by Marlene Michels Pomper, (New Jersey: Chatham House Publishers inc., 1985), p. 60.
2. Henry A. Plotkin, The Election of 1984: Reports and Interpretations, various authors, edited by Marlene Michels Pomper, (New Jersey: Chatham House Publishers inc., 1985), p. 36.
3. Gerald M. Pomper, The Election of 1984: Reports and Interpretations, various authors, edited by Marlene Michels Pomper, (New Jersey: Chatham House Publishers inc., 1985), p. 70.
4. Henry A Plotkin, The Election of 1984: Reports and Interpretations, various authors, edited by Marlene Michels Pomper, (New Jersey: Chatham House Publishers inc., 1985), p. 38.
5. Henry A Plotkin, The Election of 1984: Reports and Interpretations, various authors, edited by Marlene Michels Pomper, Chatham House Publishers inc., 1985), p. 70.
6. IBID p. 62.
7. Peter Goldman & Tony Fuller, The Quest For The Presidency 1984, (Bantam Books: Toronto, 1985), p 21.
8. IBID p. 28.

9. Scott Keeter, The Election of 1984 (New Jersey: Chatham House, 1985) p. 95.
10. William A. Henry III, Visions Of America: How We Saw The 1984 Election, (Boston: Atlantic Monthly Press, 1985), p. 3.
11. IBID.
12. Jack W. Germond and Jules Witcover, Wake Us When It's Over: Presidential Politics In 1984. (New York: Macmillan Publishing, 1985), p. 245.
13. IBID p. 542.
14. William A. Henry III, Visions Of America: How We Saw The 1984 Election, (Boston: Atlantic Monthly Press, 1985), p. 67.
15. Jack W. Germond and Jules Witcover, Wake Us When It's Over: Presidential Politics In 1984. (New York: Macmillan Publishing, 1985), p. 480.
16. Jonathan Moore, Campaign For President: The Managers Look At '84, (Dover, MA: Auburn House Publishing Co., 1986), p. XVI.
17. Keith Blume, The Presidential Election Show: Campaign 84 And Beyond On The Nightly News, (MA: Bergin and Garvey Publishers, 1985), p. 185.
18. Jack W. Germond and Jules Witcover, Wake Us When It's Over: Presidential Politics In 1984. (New York: Macmillan Publishing, 1985), p. 459.
19. William A. Henry III, Visions Of America: How We Saw The 1984 Election, (Boston: Atlantic Monthly Press, 1985), p. 67.

20. Paul R. Abramson, John Aldrich, David W. Rhode, Change And Continuity In The 1984 Elections, (Washington, DC: Congressional Quarterly Press, 1987) p. 63.
21. IBID p. 53.
22. IBID p. 56.
23. IBID p. 60.
24. IBID p. 53.
25. Harold W. Stanley, Race And Realignment, an article featured in The 1984 Presidential Election In The South, edited by Robert P. Steed, Laurence W. Moreland and Tod A. Baker, (New York: Praeger Publishers, 1986), p. 329.
26. IBID
27. IBID
28. IBID p. 310.

Chapter Three

# The Losing End: Vietnam On Film

## Shifting Shadows of War Across the Silver Screen

The Vietnam War presented quite a formidable challenge to those Hollywood filmmakers who were long accustomed to portraying American soldiers as invincible heroes, always winning in the end, militarily and morally.

Vietnam, after all, was a war the United States badly lost, a war strongly opposed by many Americans, who viewed it as pointless and dehumanizing.
In this chapter, I'll analyze the different ways the Vietnam War has been portrayed in movies and examine how these films shaped – and were shaped by – public opinion.

We'll explore attempts by filmmakers to foster various perceptions of the war through such films as 'The Green Berets' through to 'Apocalypse Now' and 'Rambo'.

Through these films and others, the filmmakers tried to structure versions of reality for millions of people who had no direct contact with the war.

Throughout the 1960s and into the 1970s, American filmmakers followed a time-honoured tradition of presenting American soldiers as heroes fighting a "good war," a war with a clearly evil enemy, a war with a justifiable cause for sending young men off to fight and die on a distant battlefield.

In most cases, the war moviemakers chose to depict on film was World War II. This "good war," was the subject of an array of films, including 'Battle of the Bulge' (1965), 'The Dirty Dozen' (1967) and 'Where Eagles Dare' (1969), to name but a few.

But the Vietnam War, with its ill-defined justification, drawn-out duration and lack of an American win, was remarkably different from past wars. There was no clear-cut good guy or bad guy. The reasons for sending boys overseas were confusing and contradictory. There was no victory, moral or otherwise.

All of this presented filmmakers with a difficult situation. Many simply refused to confront the war at all through the course of the protracted, bloody confrontation overseas. They didn't want to talk about Vietnam – let alone make a film about this ugly war.

A notable – some would say infamous – exception arrived with the 1968 release of the jingoistic film 'The Green Berets', produced by Michael Wayne and staring his father, the late actor, John Wayne.
In many ways, 'The Green Berets' treated the Vietnam War as though is was one of the world wars, complete with rugged good-guy Americans fighting a vile, beatable enemy.

This one-dimensional, simplistic treatment of a tragic, horrific and complicated war was universally condemned by movie critics, including the New York Times, which pulled no punches in offering this assessment:
> "The Green Berets is a film so unspeakable, so stupid, so rotten and false in every detail… it is vile and insane."   1.

While similarly condemning Wayne for creating such a stupid and one-sided piece of propaganda, the Washington Post simply dismissed 'The Green Berets' as "a dreadful movie."   2.

As Gilbert Adair, author of 'Vietnam on Film', notes, crowds of protesting Americans picketed movie theatres showing 'The Green Berets', a film Adair berates as having assumed a "Neanderthal hawkish stance."   3.

Adair finds 'The Green Berets' was little more than an outrageous lie. He adds:

> "What is so repugnant about 'The Green Berets' is not its politics, but the fact that – in spite of overwhelming evidence to the contrary, evidence that by the late 1960s had already filtered trough to the United States – its filmmakers were determined to reduce the Vietnam War to simple-minded Manichean antithesis: good guys versus bad guys, cowboys versus Indians, white men versus natives." 4.

'The Green Berets' altered this time-worn, simplistic formula only slightly when it introduces to the film the character of a cynical journalist (David Jannsen in a thankless role), who initially reflects the views of many Americans when he pointedly questions American involvement in the war.

Then, Jannsen's character accepts a challenge from Colonel Mike Kirby (Wayne) to see the war for himself. The viewer is then transported to scenes of American-loving Vietnamese villagers, grateful for U.S. help in fending off the hideous Viet Cong and their sadistic bamboo traps.

Adair sarcastically describes the film's portrayal of the South Vietnamese as:

> "allies displaying a faith in American goodwill so unswerving that one would have

to go back to the Liberation of Paris in 1944 to find its equal." 5.

Jannsen's journalist is converted to Wayne's hawkish views after discovering the gang rape of a child by five Viet Cong (a completely fabricated event).

Not content with this bit of purely invented sadism attributed to the Viet Cong, Wayne rubs salt in the journalist's shattered psyche by describing an earlier gang rape of a woman by 40 Viet Cong.

Adair dryly wonders how the screen writers set about inventing a sadistic event, which had no basis in reality:
"Why, for example, forty (rapists)? Was thirty considered too few? A tentatively suggested sixty laughed out of the writers' room?" 6.

Of course, the journalist character only existed in the movie so that he – and one suspects, the American public – could subsequently be converted to the U.S. military's point of view via scenes filled with invented acts of Viet Cong sadism that were also remarkably free of American atrocities.

In this manner, 'The Green Berets' tried to shape public opinion by presenting a one-sided anti-Viet Cong message.

Adair notes, this quite obvious bit of intelligence-insulting propaganda was openly rejected by scores of Americans who had seen and read news reports of atrocities, who knew the war was a complicated tragedy with mounting American death tolls.

Simply put, 'The Green Berets' was breathtaking in its audacity in its zeal to reduce the war to a simplistic cartoon populated with good-guy Americans and bad-guy Viet Cong.

In fact, 'The Green Berets' went way, way over the top with its jingoistic version of the Vietnam War. As Adair observes:

> "The offense of Wayne and son proved a dual one: not only did their movie provide a tritely simplified, almost nostalgic reading of what was in reality shot through with self-recriminations and self-exonerations, prejudice and sheer bad faith, but they attempted to impose such a reading while the war was still going on."   7.

Playboy magazine also criticized Wayne for:

> "the actor's obdurately hawkish support of the Indo-China war – as glorified in his production of 'The Green Berets', which had the dubious distinction of being probably the only pro-war movie made in Hollywood during the 'Sixties."   8.

Wayne, an untalented actor who had never fought in a real war, offered this brief defence of his movie role:
> "The potbellied liberals," he fumed, "keep putting me down as some kind of ring-wing extremist and all that crap, when all I am is a patriot." 9.

One can only hope the critics did some soul-searching after upsetting him like that.

Controversy and protests over the film spread across the U.S. and Canada and around the world. Sweden, for example, pulled 'The Green Berets' film from 550 theatres with this stated justification:
> "The film is pure propaganda." 10.

Public backlash to 'The Green Berets', combined with the complexity of a war Americans were losing, increased the reluctance of Hollywood to act on the many Vietnam War scripts being circulated in the late 1960s.

In this manner, public attitudes shaped the response – or rather lack of response – of filmmakers in the late 1960s to early 1970s.

But while many filmmakers were reluctant to make a Vietnam War movie, the war still had a way of making its presence felt.

Jay Hyams, author of 'War Movies', notes that while the Vietnam War raged on, filmmaker Robert Altman's 1970 movie M*A*S*H instead used the Korean War to deliver "the clear, topical message: war is insane."   11.

Hyams suggests M*A*S*H is one of many examples of a longstanding reluctance among filmmakers to deal directly with the Vietnam War:
> "The war in Vietnam caused a great rift in American society, and, American filmmakers, lacking a clear consensus of opinion to follow, chose to bide their time."   12.

Hyams suggests the main reason for avoiding any dealing with the war was that it was simply too painful a reality to confront:
> "To many Americans, the war in Vietnam was itself a suicide mission, an apparently endless conflict that could not be won. The Vietnam War destroyed one of the most cherished beliefs of many Americans, the belief in the infallibility of their armed forces. It was a belief engendered in large part by films: Americans were used to seeing hordes of Oriental armies mown down with ease; now they were faced with television newscasters reporting casualty figures for a war without victories."   13.

Although the Vietnam War continued to drag on until 1973, another 1970 movies, Franklin Schaffner's

'Patton', similarly utilized another way – in this case World War II – to deliver a strong statement.

With an enormous American flag draped behind him, General George S. Patton (portrayed by George C. Scott) delivers a ringing speech in which he tells his men that:
> "All this stuff you've heard about America not wanting to fight, wanting to stay out of the war, is a lot of horse dung. Americans traditionally love to fight. All real Americans love the sting of battle."     14.

As Hyams wryly notes, it was a message prominent members of a more contemporary America, involved directly with the Vietnam War, apparently took to heart. Unfortunately, it tended to be Republican politicians who were most enamoured with the movie's message:
> "The image of Patton was tarnished somewhat when it was learned that President Nixon had watched it and like it so mush that he had seen it again, just five days before ordering American forces to invade Cambodia."     15.

Even while filmmakers avoided any direct confrontation with the Vietnam War, moviegoers were themselves presented with either real or perceived Vietnam messages that at times verged on the subliminal.

Such was the case with the violent and cynical 1970 Robert Aldrich film on the Second World War, 'Too late The Hero'. As Hyams reflects:

> "Advertisements for the film showed a dead soldier lying across the word war with legend: 'It's a dying business'. The advertisement is notable because the soldier's weapon, resting on his chest, is an m-16, the weapon of Vietnam, and not World War II." 16.

One can only wonder if filmmakers were testing the waters, using indirect references to Vietnam to calculate the mood of an American public that appeared to want nothing more than for the war, and its constant yield of body bags, to come to an end as quickly as possible.

In fact, the Vietnam War was nearly over before filmmakers began to openly address it – though in a distant way, as Hyams also observes:

> "One of the last films made about the Vietnam War while it was still being fought was Limbo (1972), directed by Mark Robson. Limbo presents the emotional crises experienced by three women who husbands are either prisoners of North Vietnamese or are listed as missing in action." 17.

With Limbo, the public finally had a movie that actually focussed on the war, but not through the eyes of the Vietnamese who were there (that film is yet to be made) or through the eyes of the soldiers who fought it, but through the eyes of those who stayed at home and were indirectly affected by it.

The war's impact on Americans was a theme that would come to be repeated often through mainstream and counter-culture films from 'Welcome Home Soldier Boys' to 'Gordon's War', 'One Flew Over The Cuckoo's Nest', 'The Stone Killer', and 'Taxi Driver', all with their crazed and dangerous Vietnam veterans.

All of these films focussed not on the war itself, but rather on its bitter aftermath of difficult readjustment and return to an uncaring society. As Hyams notes:
> "The theme of most movies about returning Vietnam veterans is the same: searching for peace, they find only violence, for America is a violent place." 18.

This 1970s tendency to approach the war from every direction but head-on clearly reflected the perverse reaction filmmakers had to growing public dissention over the war.

This dissention again appears to be indicative of public opinion shaping the views of filmmakers, who in turn attempted to shape public opinion by eases the masses into the war via movies that looked at the war's edges – not its centre.

Hyams, reflecting on this wariness among filmmakers, offers this observation about 'Limbo':
> "One of the first attempts to deal with the effects of the Vietnam War on Americans, 'Limbo' was ahead of its time. Its title is an apt description of the place the Vietnam War occupied in film history during the early years of the 1970s, for there were no major films about the Vietnam War until the last years of the decade." 19.

Not that writers were asleep at the switch. As Hyams further observes:
> "There were plenty of screenplays about Vietnam making the rounds of Hollywood studios, but no one dared touch the subject. Not until 1975 when Francis Ford Coppola announced his plans to make 'Apocalypse Now' did American filmmakers show any interest in films about Vietnam." 20.

Production work delayed the release of 'Apocalypse Now' until 1979, by which time 'Coming Home' and 'The Deer Hunter' were released. As Hyams notes:
> "These films were regarded as statements – they were going to tell Americans how to feel about an event that had been central to their lives for more than a decade." 21.

'Coming Home' tried to shape public opinion against the war (which had ended five years earlier) via a range of antiwar statements from actors portraying disabled Vietnam War veterans.

Actor John Voight, in the role of a paraplegic veteran, expresses regret over killing and watching friends for his country wile overseas. And he suggests: "If we want to commit suicide we can find plenty of way to do it right here." 22.

Bruce Dern, in the role of a disillusioned, distraught marine officer admits he doesn't understand the war and was disturbed by gruesome acts of violence by his own men toward the corpses of Viet Cong. He commits suicide after discovering his wife has been unfaithful.

The focus of 'Coming Home' rarely strayed from the affect the war had on Americans who lived through it and had to readjust to society.

There is no real effort made to explain the war or depict its battles or show the war from the Vietnamese perspective.

Reflecting on the film's emphasis on the psychological toll the war had on Americans, The New York Times felt compelled to offer this observation:
"Coming Home is more about Freud, perhaps, than the war." 23.

With its relative lack of violence and immediacy, the structure of 'Coming Home' indulged mild feelings of protest against the war while leaving room for sympathy for the American soldiers who went through emotional turmoil.

In this manner, 'Coming Home' may have come closest to reflecting the dominant views of a deeply divided nation.

As Hyams points out:

> "Of all the films about Vietnam released in the late 1970s, 'Coming Home' makes the clearest anti-war statement. It was delivered of course, woefully late." 24.

In sharp contrast, Michael Cimino's 'The Deer Hunter' (1978) was a dark, deeply disturbing, powerful film, which at first focuses on a group of three American boyhood friends as they prepare to leave home for the Vietnam War.

Cimino takes care to develop a warm, intimate understanding of the three central characters' lives, leaving the viewer feeling as though they know each of them.

Abruptly, the scene jarring shifts from a steel town, Pennsylvania bar to the deafening chaos of the war where the friends are now heavily involved in fighting sadistic Viet Cong who are lobbing grenades at hapless villagers.

A short while later, the friends are captured by the Viet Cong and are held in a largely underwater bamboo cage infested with rats and human corpses.

From here, the friends are dragged by their captors into a brutal, terrifying game of Russian roulette – a pointless exercise as no real effort is made to extract any information from the captives.

The sole purpose of this exercise appears to be an effort to show how nasty the enemy can be. In fact, the Viet Cong prove to be uniformly vicious and sadistic, barely human in their unsmiling zeal for human blood and suffering.
As Adair objects that "Cimino's Viet Cong cannot even be called one-dimensional. They exist merely to objectify Occidental fears of the yellow race." 25.

The friends escape after their leader (Robert DeNiro) tricks the VC into putting extra bullets in the gun – which he then turns on his captors, killing all of them.

Cimino's gripping, tension-building cinematography, combined with superb performances from a convincing cast work to violently pull the viewer into a nightmarish world of sadistic, homicidal Viet Cong verging on the subhuman.

In a film that gave me – and likely many other viewers – nightmares, Cimino expertly uses the grim Russian roulette sequences to virtually shove the viewer into concluding American soldiers were innocent good guys pitted against a vile enemy who only existed to cause pain to others.

For a public that rejected the simple-minded anti-VC message of 'The Green Berets', Cimino offered an extremely intense, considerably more sophisticated, anti-VC message of his own, using the horrific Russian roulette scenes to drive his disturbing message home.

However, much like 'The Green Berets', Cimino's anti-VC message was heavily based on a purely invented atrocity.

> As The New York Times objected:
> "Cimino admits that the Russian roulette idea was his own invention, based on no historical evidence whatsoever." 26.

However, depictions of this gruesome death game were central to 'The Deer Hunter' and were used repeatedly to illustrate the inhumanity of an enemy who supposedly regarded human life as a cheap commodity to be snuffed out for amusement.

Adair offers this reflection on Cimino being taken to task for manipulating the audience with his purely invented atrocity:
> "When question, Cimino, shamefully acknowledging that he had never heard of such a game being played during the war, pleaded dramatic license as his was a movie about America, not Vietnam." 27.

In fact, virtually all of the widely known Vietnam movies make the Vietnamese secondary to the narrow, central theme of how Americans suffered in the war and struggled with its aftermath.

Although the Americans lost the Vietnam War and are unquestionably the political losers, their overwhelming powerful position on the world stage almost allows them to get away with rewriting history. Almost, but not quite.

To some degree, the filmmakers may simply have been reflecting the mindset – real or perceived – of a self-centred culture more concerned with protecting American interests than in reaching an meaningful understanding of the Vietnamese situation.

When legendary filmmaker Francis Ford Coppola's 'Apocalypse Now' (inspired by the work of Dispatches author Michael Herr) was finally released in 1979, it continued the trend of exploiting, as opposed to explaining, the Vietnam War.

The war was used as a backdrop to the central theme of a quest involving a hit man (Martin Sheen) touring the chaos of war while stalking renegade American Colonel Kurtz (an overblown Marlon Brando).

'Apocalypse Now' followed the now familiar pattern of telling a purely American story about, by and for Americans.

Vietnam's "natives" were again little more than props in this film.

Expressing disappointment over the film's missed opportunity to explain the war, critic Vincent Canby noted that "ultimately, 'Apocalypse Now' is neither a tone poem nor an opera. It's an adventure yarn with delusions of grandeur."   28.

Along the way, the viewer is assaulted with some spectacular battle scenes, including the memorable attack in which the trigger-happy Colonel Kilgore (Robert Duvall) descends from his 'Death From Above' helicopter to announce: "I love the smell of napalm in the morning."   29.

Canby also wonders what kind of message Coppola was trying to convey:
> "Certain critics, however, even if they admit to being dazzled by the purely visual pyrotechnics of the scene, accused Coppola of indirectly glorifying what he had presumably intended to indict."   30.

When Kurtz is finally confronted, he lays out a mad man's justification of evil which, true to form, relies on a purely invented atrocity to lend it validity. In this case the big lie involves the concocted nastiness of the Viet Cong supposedly lopping off the arms of Vietnamese children who'd been inoculated by American doctors.

Coppola may well have stripped bare the chaos, tragedy and obscenity of the Vietnam War. Any deeper messages are left open to interpretation – a task made exceedingly more difficult by the filmmaker's constant efforts to bend the truth, portray distortions as reality and generally manipulate the audience.

Oliver Stone's 'Platoon' is widely credited with finally providing movie goers with a realistic, grunt's-eye-view of the war – but not a great deal more than that. As the New York Times notes:
> "Platoon is about war as seen by men for whom the only goal is daily survival. There are no great issues here.... no debates about good and evil."  31.

Far worse than the narrow focus of some films is the wholesale distortion of others – such as Rambo – which refashion history and attempt to cram the unwieldy Vietnam War into the familiar, tired formula of the heroic 'good war' films.

And there was a new trend underway in which it was constantly suggested that although the war was lost, it should have been won – and would have been won save for government inertia. The New York Times is certainly no fan of this mid-1980s trend, offering this observation:
> "The new Vietnam films – including 'Rambo', Chuck Norris's 'Missing In Action (1984) and 'Missing In Action 2', and 'Uncommon Valor' (1983), plus segments of such TV shows as 'Magnum PI' and 'Airwolf' – don't deny that the war was lost. That's not possible. Instead, they restart the war that, they

say, the United States Government fuddy-duddies would not allow to be won 10 years ago, and, this time, score decisive, totally fictitious victories ... they are far more committed to changing history by adding new chapters to it." 32.

Kitchener author David Morrell has watched his anti-war Rambo character (who gets killed in his novel) become very badly distorted by Hollywood. Tinseltown has refashioned Rambo to transform him into a superhuman fighting machine with such little redeeming value that the British Safety Council pushed to have the second Rambo film banned, denouncing it as: "Ninety-six minutes of mindless violence." 33.

In contrast, although the Germans had their own date with disaster during the Second World War, it didn't prevent them from objectively re-examining the war through a number of soul-searching films, including 'Angry Harvest'.

Former Hamilton Spectator movie critic John Levesque offered this praise for 'Angry harvest':
"This admirably clear-eyed movie from West Germany scrutinizes human nature under the strain of nazi race hatred and war." 34.

In equally sharp contrast to such reflective and responsible German films, American filmmakers have gone from virtually ignoring the Vietnam War altogether, to timidly referring to the war in unrelated films, to dealing with the war indirectly, to finally looking at the war from a soldier's perspective – but without ever attempting to explain the history or reasons behind the war.

As Levesque notes of a growing number of Vietnam Films:
> "By now, the genre is recognizable from a hundred yards away: Vietnam films are not so much about the war itself but about the dark night of the American soul." 35.

What's needed of course, is an honest appraisal of the Vietnam War, one that sheds new light on this lengthy tragedy, one which challenges perceptions instead of indulging prejudices, one that openly admits the U.S. lost the war – then examines the reasons why and explores the war's troubled history.

Unfortunately, if U.S. filmmakers were ever headed in the direction of such a badly needed postwar examination, they have been pushed in the direction of mindless violence and hero worship through the vile 'Rambo'/Chuck Norris crush of films, which all but rewrite history in an effort to create new 'victories'.

Now, the Vietnam War is at risk of being ignored once again as Americans shift their attention to the far more appealing War on Terrorism and the Gulf War, which came complete with an absolute victory by the Americans over an unquestionably evil enemy who prompted the Americans' heroic actions when he invaded Kuwait.

The Gulf War very much fits the Hollywood formula for 'good wars' and it's a relatively safe bet filmmakers will continue to move with considerably more haste when it comes to making films based on and around this unequivocal victory.

Yet, the need for a detailed film exploration of the Vietnam War remains.

Unless the public one day obtains a clear and honest understanding of this brutal, drawn-out war, a strong risk remains that future generations will repeat the mistakes of the past.

As it stands, the United States very much remains a political loser when it comes to the Vietnam War. The ongoing failure to examine this fiasco in any meaningful or instructive way suggests little has been learned from the mistakes made.

The war dealt the U.S. a humiliating blow. It called into question American military prowess. It called into question the American role on the world stage. And it called into question the American way of life.

Despite its awesome might, despite the fact that it remains a political winner in most other respects, the U.S. has been unable to successfully refashion the Vietnam War into anything resembling a victory of any kind. Indeed, filmmakers efforts in this regard have met with ridicule and contempt. Nor has the victory of the Gulf War erased the painful loss of the Vietnam War.

When it comes to meaningful reflections on the Vietnam War, the U.S. is destined to be forever cast as a political loser in that very costly conflict.

# End Notes:

1. Renate Adler, New York Times, July 23, 1968. p. 21.
2. William Rice, Washington Post, July 22, 1968. p. 22.
3. Gilbert Adair, Vietnam on Film: From The Green Berets to Apocalypse Now, 1981. Proteus Publishing Co. Inc., New York, New York, p. 35.
4. Gilbert Adair, Vietnam on Film: From The Green Berets to Apocalypse Now, 1981. Proteus Publishing Co. Inc., New York, New York, p. 35.
5. Gilbert Adair, Vietnam on Film: From The Green Berets to Apocalypse Now, 1981. Proteus Publishing Co. Inc., New York, New York, p. 49.
6. Gilbert Adair, Vietnam on Film: From The Green Berets to Apocalypse Now, 1981. Proteus Publishing Co. Inc., New York, New York, p. 37.
7. Gilbert Adair, Vietnam on Film: From The Green Berets to Apocalypse Now, 1981. Proteus Publishing Co. Inc., New York, New York, p. 36.
8. Richard Warren Lewis, Playboy magazine, September 1970, p. 75.

9. Paul King, The Hamilton Spectator, June 30, 1973. p. D1.
10. Reuters, USA, July 25, 1968, as published in The Spectator on the same date, p. 22.
11. Jay Hyams, War Movies. 1984. W. H. Smith. New York, New York. p. 183.
12. Jay Hyams, War Movies. 1984. W. H. Smith. New York, New York. p. 183.
13. Jay Hyams, War Movies. 1984. W. H. Smith. New York, New York. p. 183.
14. Jay Hyams, War Movies. 1984. W. H. Smith. New York, New York. p. 184.
15. Jay Hyams, War Movies. 1984. W. H. Smith. New York, New York. p. 185.
16. Jay Hyams, War Movies. 1984. W. H. Smith. New York, New York. p. 195.
17. Jay Hyams, War Movies. 1984. W. H. Smith. New York, New York. p. 195.
18. Jay Hyams, War Movies. 1984. W. H. Smith. New York, New York. p. 195.
19. Jay Hyams, War Movies. 1984. W. H. Smith. New York, New York. p. 195.
20. Jay Hyams, War Movies. 1984. W. H. Smith. New York, New York. p. 194.
21. Jay Hyams, War Movies. 1984. W. H. Smith. New York, New York. p. 198.
22. Jay Hyams, War Movies. 1984. W. H. Smith. New York, New York. p. 199.
23. Vincent Canby, New York Times, Feb. 18, 1978. p. 172.
24. Jay Hyams, War Movies. 1984. W. H. Smith.

New York, New York. p. 199.
25. Gilbert Adair, Vietnam on Film: From The Green Berets to Apocalypse Now, 1981. Proteus Publishing Co. Inc., New York, New York, p. 139.
26. Vincent Canby, New York Times, December 17, 1978. p. 262.
27. Gilbert Adair, Vietnam on Film: From The Green Berets to Apocalypse Now, 1981. Proteus Publishing Co. Inc., New York, New York, p. 137.
28. Vincent Canby, New York Times, August 15, 1979. p. 84.
29. Gilbert Adair, Vietnam on Film: From The Green Berets to Apocalypse Now, 1981. Proteus Publishing Co. Inc., New York, New York, p. 153.
30. Gilbert Adair, Vietnam on Film: From The Green Berets to Apocalypse Now, 1981. Proteus Publishing Co. Inc., New York, New York, p. 151.
31. Vincent Canby, New York Times, Jan. 11, 1987. p. 4.
32. Vincent Canby, New York Times, May 24, 1985, p. 4.
33. Associated Press, Hamilton Spectator, Aug. 6, 1989. p. A14.
34. John Levesque, Hamilton Spectator, Feb. 24, 1989, p. E1.
35. John Levesque, Hamilton Spectator, August 18, 1989. p. E1.

The following chapter examines the relationships of food, famine and power in Ukraine as elements in Moscow's efforts to put down Ukrainian nationalism and exert full control over her resources and people.

"...A very good essay..."
- McMaster University Political Science Professor Dr. Peter Potichnyj.

Chapter Four

# Killing Fields: Ukraine's Forced Famine

Even eye witnesses had difficulty describing the horrific nightmare of twisted, starved corpses that littered the Ukrainian countryside following Moscow's deliberately created forced famine of 1932-1933.

Ukrainian Famine survivor Miron Dolot, author of Execution By Hunger, was sickened by the sight of men driven to acts of cannibalism and madness and of children hovering between life and death. As Dolot recalls:

> "The bodies of some were reduced to skeletons, with their kin handing greyish-yellow and loose over their bones. Their faces looked like rubber masks with large, bulging, immobile eyes. Their necks seemed to have shrunk into their shoulders. The look in their eyes was glassy, heralding their approaching death." 1.

This was the man-made famine created by Iosif Vissarionovich Djugashvili – known to the world as Josef Stalin.

The famine was Stalin's genocidal version of Hitler's 'Final Solution' and with total deaths estimated at between five-million and 10-million people, it produced results every bit as cruel and inhuman as the Jewish Holocaust.

So successful was Stalin in keeping this deliberate disaster a secret from the West, it was years before many people in the West would even accept that it had happened.

Even today, the Great Famine remains something of a hidden holocaust to many Canadians who remain unaware of the enormous scale of this bitter and sadistic man-made tragedy.

Fewer still are aware that the 1932-1933

famine was not the first time Moscow used starvation as a weapon against Ukrainians to suppress their struggle for nationhood and seize absolute control of the country's rich natural resources.

As this chapter, based on extensive research and numerous sources, will show, a heavily centralized and ruthless Moscow has repeatedly used famine as a weapon of oppression against helpless civilian populations.

The famines in Ukraine are all the more unforgivable given Ukraine's historic and normal status as the breadbasket of Europe, producing as much as a third of all the grain harvested annually in the former Soviet Union. Ukraine is also rich in minerals.

The first known man-made famine to hit Ukraine, in 1921-1923, took place under Lenin's leadership and was followed by the massive 1932-1933 famine, which was in turn followed by the 1946-1947 famine.

As writer Roman Serbyn notes, the 1921-1923 famine began of natural causes in Russia. But in Ukraine, the famine was largely caused by Lenin's 1921 orders to simply confiscate as much grain from Ukraine as Russia needed, regardless of the impact on the population of the then-sovereign Ukraine. As Serbyn observes:

> "The 1921 famine in Russia was caused by natural calamities, albeit aggravated

by the regime's economic and political policies. In Ukraine, it was brought about primarily by excessive taxation and outright plunder. The drought prevented the peasants from replenishing confiscated stores. In Russia, nature was the chief cause of famine, whereas in Ukraine, the State was responsible." 2.

Serbyn also states that while as many as 2-million Ukrainians died in the 1921-1923 famine, Soviet authorities ignored the death toll and continued to confiscate food and taxes to help Russia.

The Soviet authorities confiscated food from Ukraine, knowing the country was starving.

As well, they denied outside help to Ukraine by deliberately delaying internal and international aid to Ukraine in an effort to crush the country's independent spirit and exert full control over the lives of Ukrainians. Serbyn notes:

"For Moscow, the famine was a blessing in disguise. It was an effective way of crushing Ukrainian peasant resistance to the Soviet regime and it was a powerful weapon against the peasant-supported armed rebels. Startled by the famine in Russia, the Soviet Authorities decided to exploit its merits in Ukraine. Stalin had a model for his own ventures ten years later." 3.

But if Stalin needed a reminder of the effectiveness of starvation as a weapon, he got such a reminder with the 1930 forced famine in Kazakhstan.

Rather than see their herds come under state control through collectivization, Kazakh herdsmen slaughtered their livestock – and Moscow saw an opportunity.

As political observer J. E. Mace notes:
"Rather than extend them aid, the regime decided to teach them a lesson by letting them starve. So many died that the 1939 Soviet census shows 21.9 per cent fewer Kazakhs in the USSR than there had been in 1926. But resistance among them ceased. The lesson was obvious. Famine could be a highly effective weapon."   4.

Just two years later, Stalin inflicted a far greater man-made famine on an unsuspecting Ukraine.

Alex DeJonge, author of 'Stalin', points out that Stalin, in running the USSR, headed a massive political federation covering one sixth of the Earth's land mass.

Yet, as DeJonge also observes, the Soviet leader had little tolerance for deviations from his central government's policies, despite the fact that these policies applied to a vast, broad empire encompassing more than 200 different languages and some 300-million people.

That Stalin would go to the extremes of inflicting famine on literally millions of people is less surprising when one examines the character of the man that DeJonge describes as ruthless, cold-blooded, intolerant, paranoid and power-hungry.

DeJonge depicts Stalin as a heartless tyrant without a shred of compassion or mercy:
> "There is no evidence that Stalin loved anyone... he would refer to his mother in appalling terms – for example, as: 'that old whore'." 5.

Nor is there much evidence of Stalin ever respecting human rights or the sovereign right of countries to govern themselves.

Stalin was arguably even more vicious than Adolph Hitler with whom he shares a number of interesting parallels, not the least of which is that both men led countries they were not natives of. Just as Hitler wasn't German (he was Austrian), Stalin wasn't Russian (he was Georgian).

Like Hitler, Stalin seized control of his native country on behalf of a powerful neighbouring country he would come to control. Stalin took over Georgia on behalf of Moscow by engineering a Red Army-assisted uprising in a then-sovereign Georgia in 1921, taking control after three weeks of bloody fighting that left many of his countrymen – including his next-door neighbours – dead.

Indeed, in referring to Stalin's deep-rooted

contempt for his native Georgia, DeJonge describes the freely murderous, barbaric dictator as a man "whose dislike of Tiflis (his home town) was almost as great as Hitler's loathing of Vienna." 6.

Given Stalin's brutal treatment of his own birthplace, his heavy-handed extreme effort to control and assimilate – or Russify – Ukraine is less surprising than it might first appear.

Stalin was always ready to act viciously on the principle that any nation unable to defend itself should be assimilated.

Not that Stalin's measures met with no resistance. But with every peasant-led uprising in Ukraine, he simply worked harder and more ruthlessly to bring the nation under his thumb.

An early major effort to control Ukraine came with the move to collectivization – or absolute state control – of Ukrainian farmland under a system initiated by Moscow in 1928.

Collectivization ended a post-Civil War period of relative independence in Ukraine when farmers had been free to won their land and control their own production even though prices were set by the state.

DeJonge notes Stalin favoured the absolute control offered by collectivization, in part, because he viewed the independent and efficient peasant-farmers as a threat to the Soviet Union and his own growing power.

Since the peasants initially controlled food production by virtue of their farming efforts, Stalin saw the very act of food production as a threat. The dictator used collectivization as a means of controlling the peasantry. As DeJonge observes:

> "He believed that the peasantry had the ability to hold the (Communist) party to ransom by withholding food from the marketplace... In the second place, the peasantry fell largely outside Soviet rule and might be thought of as offering an eventual threat to the regime via the Red Army. Stalin envisioned collectivization as a means of consolidating and extending the authority of the party by purging an opposition." 7.

In addition to bringing the peasant population under control, Stalin soon saw collectivization as a means of extracting as much grain and other agricultural products as possible, not only for Russia's use, but also for export, enabling the Soviet Union to obtain the necessary hard currency to fund its first five-year plan for industrialization.

But the system, largely run by incompetent young bureaucrats ignorant of agriculture, was virtually guaranteed to fail as it meant complete state ownership of land and farm production along with outrageously high production quotas that left little grain (or incentive) for the farmers themselves to subsist on and little money in return for their efforts.

Stripped of ownership of their land and without any claim to the fruits of their labour, the peasants understandably did not produce at high levels.
With success punished and the profit incentive eliminated, production fell.
Moscow retaliated.
As Harvard University research director Adam Ulam points out:
> "Instead of adopting what would have been the commonsense solution to the problem, i.e., raising prices paid to the producers, the government embarked on a drastic campaign against the peasantry as a class. They were to be coerced and regimented so that they would become not merely employees, but virtual slaves of the state, just as their ancestors in Imperial Russia before 1861 had been serfs of individual landlords. The machinery for that transformation was to be collectivization. The individual holdings of some 25-million peasant households were to be amalgamated in approximately 250,000 collective and state farms." 8.

But the quotas remained high as Stalin continued to collect every possible speck of grain – most of it sold to foreign countries to raise hard currency –

and literally left the farmers with nothing, As DeJonge notes:

> "The 1932 harvest was a poor one, about 12 per cent below average, but the grain was needed to finance the plan even though this entailed selling into a falling market. Grain exports had risen from 200,000 tons in 1928 to nearly 5-million tons in 1931." 9.

Even after Stalin received reports of widespread famine in Ukraine, he continued to deny its existence to the outside world to prevent aid from ever reaching many millions of starving people.

The West was largely taken in by this ruthless dictator, in part, because Stalin pointed to the Soviet Union's record grain exports as evidence there was an abundance of food. Of course, none of this food ever made it back to the farmers who planted it.

So-called rich peasants – or Kulaks – were at times murdered by jealous party officials and co-opted villagers, while any peasant who took some of his own grain to eat was guilty of theft against the state and was severely punished by Soviet officials.

Even after the streets filled with starved corpses, a legion of ardent Stalin followers continued to insist there were hidden reserves of grain. These followers insisted that the dying peasants were deliberately starving themselves rather than disclose locations of non-existent stores of hidden grain.

Given the mounting death toll, the assertions of hidden grain defied all logic – but that didn't stop local party officials from launching another crackdown. Ulam notes:

> "With official blessing, the village riffraff was incited to acts of violence against the kulaks. They and their families were beaten and thrown out of their home, men lynched and property plundered." 10.

Reliving his own horrific survival memories, Dolot recalls:

> "We couldn't help feeling that we pawns in some lethal game. Each of our moves to escape death met with an official countermove; each of our measures to avert it was opposed with official countermeasures. In their opposition and retaliation against us, the officials often resorted to actions that would have been ridiculous but for their unbelievable sadism." 11.

Even eating spilled grain off the ground was considered a sin against the State. As Dolot adds:

> "It was considered a great crime to even glean the already-harvested fields, to fish in the rivers, or to pick up some dry branches in the forest for firewood... everything was considered socialist, state-owned property, and thus, was protected by law." 12.

Dolot is among many Ukrainians who feel this inhuman persecution of the peasants, the brutal treatment, the withholding of food to the starving and cynical denials of any famine, all added up to a sinister plot to crush Ukraine to Russia's will.

Certainly the orchestrated pain and suffering bore all the earmarks of a conspiracy and a planned destruction of a people. To Dolot, there was nothing unintentional about the widespread devastation brought about by Moscow's destructive measures. He asserts:

> "It finally became clear to us that there was a conspiracy against us; that somebody wanted to annihilate us, not only as farmers, but as a people – as Ukrainians." 13.

Ukrainian writer Bohdan Krawchenko also emphasizes the deliberate nature of the famine and the extreme measures taken by officials to maximize the suffering. According to Krawchenko:

> "What is important to stress about the 1932-1933 famine is that was artificially created and that no effort was made to relieve the plight of its victims. When Ukraine was famine-stricken, the Soviet region exported 1.7-million tonnes of grain to the West." 14.

Krawchenko notes Stalin and Moscow were unswerving in their determination to inflict maximum pain without relief:

> "The offers of international relief organizations to assist the starving were rejected on the grounds that there was no famine in Ukraine and hence no need to aid its vic-

tims. Moreover, the borders of Ukraine were closely patrolled, and starving Ukrainian peasants were not allowed to cross into Russia in search of bread." 15.

How did so many in the regime, at the village level and among members of the peasantry themselves come to pursue such barbaric actions against Ukrainian people?

DeJonge offers a possible explanation:
"Stalin created a system that worked because people worked it, willingly, for privilege, out of idealism, out of hatred for their neighbours, and sometimes out of love." 16.

At first, the man-made famine appeared to have achieved Stalin's evil goal of bringing Ukraine firmly under his thumb. W. W. Isajiw, author of The Famine And Ukrainian Society, makes this observation:
"The main long-range consequence was that the famine removed the social vase of the Ukrainian elite of the time ... the term refers to groups of people who are able to exercise power or influence the development of political, social and cultural institutions. These are the groups of people who are an active minority and are able to achieve the goals, which they articulate by mobilizing the passive majority." 17.

However, in 1989 the Berlin Wall came crashing

down and a new and vocal Ukrainian minority emerged to promote to the new generations of Ukrainians its goals and desire for full independence from Moscow. On December 1, 1991, this goal was achieved when Ukraine obtained its independence from the former USSR.

In short order, the Soviet Union's collapse was complete and the Warsaw Pact was disbanded.

In the years leading up to, and following, Ukrainian independence, the Great Famine, long covered up by Russia and previously disbelieved by many in the West, finally began receiving increased recognition as a deliberate genocidal act against Ukraine.

Cracks in Moscow's very carefully orchestrated cover-up first began widening in the early 1980s. Marco Carynnyk author of Blind Eye To Murder, notes the former Soviet Union was dismayed by Canada's 1983 public recognition of the 1932-1933 famine:

> "... the Soviet Embassy in Ottawa attacked Brian Mulroney, the Progressive Conservative leader, for repeated "a 100 per cent lie," in reminding a commemorative rally in Toronto that the famine was "man-made, orchestrated and directed from Moscow." 18.

Gradually, however, eyes became opened to the horrors of the Ukrainian Famine and the world began to accept that Stalin has likely surpassed Hitler as the greatest mass murderer humanity has ever known.

By the late 1980s, the famine was also receiving wider recognition in the Soviet Union itself, as noted in a 1989 edition of the Soviet Nationality Survey:

> "In the first three years of Mikhail Gorbachev's regime, the question of the Ukrainian forced famine remained a taboo for the glasnost suffused news and opinion media. The ice encrusting this tragedy, however, seems to have broken... when Ukrainian Writers' Union secretary and conference delegate Boris Oliynik addressed the meeting with a stirring appeal to honour the memory of millions of victims who perished." 19.

The Soviet Nationality Survey also cites further evidence of growing public interest in the historic tragedy, including the publicity surrounding a research project and book on the famine by Ukrainian newspaper Sil-ski Visti along with a major published essay entitled '1933: The Tragedy of the Famine' in Literaturna Ukrainia by Professor Stanislav Kul-Chytsky, before concluding:

> "These developments are but an indication that a basic change in Soviet attitudes toward a hidden... aspect of national relations in the USSR is about to be felt in the fields of nationality studies..." 20.

In an article published prior to the collapse of the USSR, the Ukrainian Review makes it clear that Ukrainians are not about to forget the years of oppression and exploitation under a succession of Soviet leaders, through Lenin, Stalin and Brezhnev:

> "Moscow's policy towards the national

minorities has always been cruel, not only prior to October 1917, but later too. In the past 70 years, relations with all the nations which comprise this empire were built on coercion, the aim of which has been the physical and spiritual destruction of entire nations." 21.

Commenting further on what can be seen as primarily Russian-based oppression, the Ukrainian Review further notes:
> "In the 1930s, millions of Ukrainians were destroyed by an artificially created famine, in the 1940s, Soviet tanks trampled on the freedom of the Baltic states and western Ukraine; other nationalities were deported and met their end in Siberia." 22.

But in its relentless oppression of Ukraine, the centralized Moscow government inflicted incentive-destroying collectivization and state-controlled systems on a nation that had been relatively self-sufficient when allowed the basic freedoms of control over one's own production and land use.

In short, Moscow's efforts to take control of Ukraine and command its agricultural base were not only brutal, they simply didn't work. As the Ukrainian Review notes, Moscow's efforts were, at best, counterproductive:
> "The epilogue of all these reorganizational manoeuvres followed in 1963, when Russia, once an important grain export country, had to import grain from the

United States, Canada and other capitalist lands to avert a serious food shortage on her home front." 23.

All of this ineptitude and oppression led to a movement in Ukraine to allow Ukrainians control over their own production and resources. This movement had as its central goal, the complete and full restoration of Ukrainian statehood – and this goal was ultimately realized in 1991.

In the years leading up to restoration of Ukrainian statehood, growing throngs of Ukrainians and many political observers soon came to openly blame the centralized policies of Moscow for not only overtly oppressing, controlling and exploiting Ukrainians, but also for severely undermining Ukraine's economic health. According to Canadian writer David Marples in his Radio Liberty: Report on the USSR:

"There is a growing consensus that Ukraine's economic and ecological problems are largely the result of the violation of the sovereign rights of the republic. In short, the central authorities are said to have exploited Ukraine's resources in a manner that was not only irrational and careless but that also brought little real benefit to Ukrainians. Ukraine has been contributing far more to the budget of the USSR than it's received." 25.

There is no question that the forced famine's that killed millions also rendered Ukraine a political loser: Years after the famines ended, more than half the Ukrainian population continued to live in abject poverty. Although Ukraine was touted as an important part of the former Soviet Union, in reality, Ukraine subsisted in the role of a conquered nation with no control over its production and resources, a virtual slave to Moscow's wishes.

However, Russia and the former USSR can also be deemed political losers. The extreme domination and oppression of Ukraine and other nations by the Moscow-centred former Soviet Union was so horrific, it incited normally law-abiding citizens to rise up against their oppressors and challenge authority. The inhuman forced-famines and political crackdowns forever drove a wedge between Moscow and Ukraine and the other non-Russian members of the late USSR.

When the Soviet economy began to falter, it proved, form many, to be the final straw. Any sense of loyalty to the USSR had long been erased by ill treatment – and the many informal uprisings began to make their presence felt and bring about real change.

Ultimately, such uprisings resulted in the collapse of the USSR and the disbanding of the Warsaw Pact. Had the people been treated with greater humanity, the Soviet empire might still exist today.

Indeed, rather than crush the independent spirit of Ukraine, Stalin appears to have sown the seeds for Ukrainian independence.

Political loser Ukraine has achieved a major victory in recovering its lost statehood. It now remains to be seen if Ukraine can ever fully recover from the abuses of the past and regain its once-envied agricultural prosperity.

# End Notes/Bibliography
## For Chapter Four

1. Dolot, Miron, Execution by Hunger, WW Norton & Co., New York, 1985. p. 204.
2. Serbyn, Roman, The Famine of 1921-1923, from Famine in Ukraine, edited by Roman Serbyn and Bohdan Krawchenko, Canadian Institute of Ukrainian Studies, University of Alberta. Edmonton: 1986. p. 170.
3. IBID
4. Mace, J. E., The Man-made Famine of 1933, from Famine in Ukraine, edited by Roman Serbyn and Bohdan Krawchenko, Canadian Institute of Ukrainian Studies, University of Alberta. Edmonton: 1986. p. 6.
5. DeJonge, Alex, Stalin and the Shaping of the Soviet Union, Fontana/Collins. Glasgow, Scotland: 1986. p. 24.
6. IBID, p. 165
7. Ulam, Adam, Introduction, Execution by Hunger, WW Norton & Co., New York, 1985. p. VIII.
8. DeJonge, Alex, Stalin and the Shaping of the Soviet Union, Fontana/Collins. Glasgow, Scotland: 1986. p. 287.
9. Ulam, Adam, Introduction, Execution by Hunger, WW Norton & Co., New York, 1985. p. IX.
10. Dolot, Miron, Execution by Hunger, WW Norton & Co., New York, 1985. p. 151.
11. IBID, p. 157
12. IBID
13. IBID, p. 175.

14. Krawchenko, Bohdan, The Man-made Famine of 1932-1933, from Famine in Ukraine, edited by Roman Serbyn and Bohdan Krawchenko, Canadian Institute of Ukrainian Studies, University of Alberta. Edmonton: 1986. p. 23.
15. IBID
16. DeJonge, Alex, Stalin and the Shaping of the Soviet Union, Fontana/Collins. Glasgow, Scotland: 1986. p. 517.
17. Isajiw, W. W., The Famine and Ukrainian Society, from Famine in Ukraine, edited R. Serbyn and B. Krawchenko, Canadian Inst. of Ukrainian Studies, 1986. p. 140.
18. Carynnyk, Marco, Blind Eye to Murder, from Famine in Ukraine, edited by Roman Serbyn and Bohdan Krawchenko, Canadian Institute of Ukrainian Studies, U. of Alberta. Edmonton: 1986. p. 111.
19. Soviet Nationality Survey: Ukrainian Famine Acknowledged, Survey Vol. VI, No. 2, February 1989. p. 2.
20. IBID.
21. The Ukrainian Review, Vol. XXXVII. No. 3, Autumn 1989, p. 80.
22. IBID.
23. IBID.
24. IBID
25. IBID
26. Marples, David, Radio Liberty: Report on USSR: Vol. 2, No. 29. July 20 1990. p17.

# Bibliography

Abramson, Paul R., Aldrich, John and Rhode, David W., Change And Continuity In The 1984 Elections, Washington, DC, 1987.

Blume, Keith, The Presidential Election Show: Campaign 84 And Beyond On The Nightly News, MA: Bergin and Garvey, 1985

Brebner, J.B,, New England's Outpost: Acadia Before the Conquest of Canada, New York: Columbia University Press, 1927.

Campbell, Duncan, Nova Scotia and its Historical, Mercantile and Industrial Relations, John Lovell and Sons, 1873.

Clarke, George Frederick, Expulsion of the Acadians, Brunswick Press, 1955.

Daigle, Jean, Historical Synthesis: 1604-1763. The Acadians of the Maritimes, Centre d'etudes acadiennes, Moncton, NB, 1982.

Eccles, W. J., France in America, Harper and Row, 1972.

Francis, Douglas R., and Donald B., Readings in Canadian History: Pre Confederation, Holt, Rinehart and Winston, 1990.

Germond, Jack W., and Witcover, Jules, Wake Us When It's Over: Presidential Politics In 1984. N.Y. Macmillan, 1985.

Glynn, Lenny, Ferraro's Possible Dream, Maclean's Magazine, July 23, 1984.

Goldman, Peter, & Fuller, Tony, The Quest For The Presidency 1984, Bantam, TO: 1985.

Griffiths, Naomi, E.S., The Acadian Deportation: Deliberate Perfidy or Cruel Necessity?, Copp Clark, Toronto, 1969.

Griffiths, Naomi, E.S., The Golden Age: Acadian Life, 1713-1748, Social History 17, 33 (May 1984).

Hannay, James, The History of Acadia from its First Discovery to its Surrender to England, J&A McMillan, St. John, NB, 1879.

Henry, William, A. III, Visions Of America: Boston: Atlantic Monthly Press, 1985.

Keeter, Scott, The Election of 1984, New Jersey: Chatham House, 1985.

Kellerman, Barbara, The Political Presidency: The Practice Of Leadership From Kennedy Through Reagan, New York: Oxford University Press, 1984.
LeFeber, Walter, America, Russia And The Cold War, New York: Cornell Press, 1985.

Moore, Jonathan, Campaign For President: The Managers Look At '84, Dover, MA: Auburn House Publishing Co., 1986.

Plotkin, Henry A., and Pomper, Gerald, M., The Election of 1984: Reports and Interpretations, various authors, edited by

Marlene Michels Pomper, New Jersey: Chatham House Publishers inc., 1985.

Richard, Edouard, Acadia: Missing Links of a Lost Chapter in American history, New York Home Book Company, John Lovell and Son, Montreal, 1985.

Stanley, Harold W., The 1984 Presidential Election In The South, edited by Robert P.
Steed, Laurence W. Moreland and Tod A. Baker, New York: Praeger Publishers, 1986.

Vogler, David J., The Politics Of Congress, Toronto: Allyn and Bacon, 1988.

Webster, John Clarence, Acadia and the End of the Seventeenth Century, Tribune Press, Sackville, NB, 1934.

Manor House Publishing
(905) 648-2193

www.ingramcontent.com/pod-product-compliance
Lightning Source LLC
Chambersburg PA
CBHW031257290426
44109CB00012B/615